THE JONKHEER'S WIFE

by

John F. Landrum

To Hennine
I heard of your experience
from Jo Kerr

authorHOUSE®

John F. Landrum
April 2010

AuthorHouse™
1663 Liberty Drive, Suite 200
Bloomington, IN 47403
www.authorhouse.com
Phone: 1-800-839-8640

This book is a work of fiction. People, places, events, and situations are the product of the author's imagination. Any resemblance to actual persons, living or dead, or historical events, is purely coincidental.

First published by AuthorHouse 8/13/2007

ISBN: 978-1-4343-1778-0 (sc)

Library of Congress Control Number: 2007904118

Printed in the United States of America
Bloomington, Indiana

This book is printed on acid-free paper.

Dedication

To Martha, Sarah, and George

MEN OF HISTORY
May 14, 1940

The Panzer column rumbled on the high road. The ground, the trees, the thatch-topped houses, the cattle and windmills no longer defensible ahead, seemed to shudder, like the roll of thunder between two bolts. From the lead tank Colonel Erwin Schell, warlike as Hektor, lowered his binoculars.

Schrecklichkeit. The word stayed in his mind, a lyric to the tread's metallic screech. How long had he preached it? If you fight at all, fight terrifyingly. Fight with extreme violence.

Blitzkrieg. He rolled the "b" and the "l" in his lips, mouthing them till the word was his own. He knew the British invented the word to mock his countrymen. But lightning war described it perfectly: artillery, planes, tanks and infantry moving as one to sweep

1

an opponent shockingly back. So let them mock. The British always mock what they fear.

Germany was re-emerging as the greatest power on Earth. His countrymen's tunics flapped in the sun, men of one soul, proud and alert in column: the idea of Nation made startlingly real. History's purpose unfolding.

Inside the turret, his feet balanced on the shaking rung. He studied the roadside Netherlanders who had not evacuated, and drank vindication from their grudging surprise. For four days his tanks had run wild in Brabant. Today they crossed the great rivers to make a recruiting and training center north of the Rhine.

He wondered how many, how many, finish their years on Earth never tasting the fulfillment he knew at this moment, like a prism refracting the lights of History, Nation, and career. After Poland, Field Marshal Von Rundstedt had personally decorated him in Berlin. Now further honors would come. His Nation's eyes were on him.

A lone doubt clouded his brilliant day: still no sign of Guse, Kessler, Zimmer, Strohn and Vogel.

The clank of machine parts broke through the dimming engine hum. Why was the column slowing?

From ahead in the line his adjutant, Captain Nagel, approached. "We've found a headquarters, Colonel."

With gloved hands Erwin lifted himself from the hatch, jumped to the ground and strode to the twin-flagged Mercedes. Nagel drove him through the stone and brick houses of ancient Rhenen, the car's bright-red swastika banners pulsing in the wind like darting hounds. From the villagers' look of shock, they might have imagined the car carried the *Führer* himself.

The Mercedes left Rhenen through the city's western limit. Soon after, just a half kilometer to the west, Nagel eased into a long circle driveway, stopped the sedan and opened Erwin's door. Stepping out, Erwin studied the white brick mansion. Three rows of black shutters marked the three floors like honor guards. Beneath its ornamental balcony, three center arches graced a massive front door. The house's eastern wall opened onto a balcony with a bleached awning of red-and-white stripes; he imagined little parties of sunset cocktails. In the roof's center an ivory triangle housed a marble Athena.

Erwin walked with eyes forward, paying no attention to the dark-haired woman and the two children holding hands on the lawn. Nagel opened the thick front door. Erwin felt the air cooler inside, as his sight adjusted to the dimmed light. "I'll look for an office," he said to Nagel. "You find a bedroom."

Erwin found a library lit by giant paned windows. An ancient desk sat on a Turkish rug that covered the stone floor. He thought he recognized a Vermeer painting. On a mahogany table rested a black phonograph machine; was that Pachelbel's *Canon* fading off the still-spinning disk?

Minutes must have passed, as Erwin imagined himself at work in this place. Then he noticed Nagel.

"This will be the office," Erwin said. "Look, a phonograph. Do you have the case?"

"Just here."

"Find Sibelius."

Nagel placed a vinyl disk on the turntable. *Finlandia* vibrated the window glass as Erwin's fingers drummed the sill, Erwin studying the fields outside, like Flanders but unscarred.

His mother had died as she had given him birth. In the Great War his father had left Erwin and his older sister to an aunt, and gone to fight the English, a captain in the Kaiser's *Wehrmacht*. Erwin still remembered the telegram: his father dead of wounds after a single month in Flanders.

Before the war ended in 1918, seventeen-year-old Erwin had taken his father's place of honor, and the proud memories were still undimmed in 1940. Erwin had led a raid through barbed wire into British trenches, and his small group destroyed the better part of a larger English unit. For this action he won the *Ritter Kreuz*.

Weeks later, he ventured alone into No Man's Land under heavy fire to retrieve his wounded major. There he surprised an English platoon, shot the first three who attacked, then accepted the others' surrender. This feat won the highest honor: the *Pour le Mérite* at a ceremony in Berlin.

Now he fingered the eight-pointed cross at the base of his throat. Erwin Rommel, bringing *Blitzkrieg* to France this very moment, had also won the *Pour le Mérite*. And Erwin had seen the medal on Ludendorff and Goering in photographs. How many others shared the highest honor?

The days of glory had ended in a quick, bleak dusk. At Versailles, the English and French reduced the German army to a silly police force. Erwin had joined a training center near Kiel to teach elite squads. In those gray days, the bright victories of 1940 had been no more than a desperate dream.

Erwin could fire pistol and rifle with machine accuracy. But at Kiel, he decided a man learned more about himself and his opponent from fighting hand-to-hand, so he studied fencing and became an expert. Now, even as a Panzer commander, he wore a sword in its scabbard, his link to ancient warriorship.

Nagel interrupted his reverie. "Colonel, the woman who lives here ..."

Erwin almost asked Nagel to make her wait. Resigned, he turned instead and followed into the hallway where Nagel introduced the dark-haired woman: "Colonel Schell, this is Frau Vaubin van Dordrecht."

Erwin forgot the woman's name as Nagel voiced it. There was no hope that the conversation might be pleasant, so he began. "It will be necessary to use your home as a headquarters. Lieutenant Nagel will see to your lodging, here at your home if possible."

"I have something to show you," she answered.

Already he was losing patience with this woman. Her little issues would be for Nagel to handle, not Erwin. "It's a bad time . . ."

She seemed not to hear him, but turned and walked. Without further thought Erwin followed her, down a long hallway into a guest room where Lieutenant Reinhard Guse lay on the bed, his abdomen dressed with bloody gauze.

The floor-length curtains were fully open; curls of dust floated in the light. Erwin pulled a chair toward Guse's bed. "What happened?"

Guse swallowed dryly. "I'd have thought you were no more than a day behind us."

"If everyone had kept his bridge open as you did, we could have crossed before the surrender."

"We swam the Maas, the Waal, and the Rhine."

"No small accomplishment."

"We blacked our faces and reached the Rhine bridge unseen. We cut the detonation wires, then separated to hide until you could clear the rivers and reach us."

"Yes."

"I don't know what time I found this place. I hid behind a haystack in the barn. The dusty, corn smell of the hay is still in my nose. I feel like a goat to this minute."

Erwin made a slight smile and nodded encouragement.

Guse's voice cracked as he spoke. "I'd have never believed I could fall asleep, but I must have. I'm not sure if it was daylight yet, but suddenly a little man was standing over me with a pitchfork. The man held it overhead, and started shouting."

Erwin strained to imagine a farmer, or anyone, holding a pitchfork over the giant Guse.

"Before I could think, I tried to rise and unholster my pistol. It seemed I moved in slow motion, like a bad dream, caught between the wall and the hay. Before I could do anything, the man rammed the pitchfork into my abdomen."

Guse lowered the gauze to show Erwin the stitches. It was hard to judge how deep the wound ran.

"Then the man ran away." Guse looked outside, then back at Erwin. "I was rolling in pain. I felt a little sick to see my own blood flowing; my vision began to narrow, and my ears rang."

Guse paused.

"There's no shame in how you react to a wound."

"The next thing I knew, I woke in this bed with the stitches already in."

Suddenly the woman spoke; Erwin jumped slightly at her voice. "The man was Bart van Oostveen," she said. "The dairyman who uses our pasture."

Erwin turned to face her. "I didn't think you were still here."

"I was just outside. Sorry if I startled you."

"What were you saying?"

"The man who wounded your lieutenant: he's just a dairyman. He was shocked to find your lieutenant in his hay-barn. He's still hiding, terrified of some reprisal."

"Why? The battle's over."

"Can I tell him it's safe to come back?"

What a question. "Of course."

"Your word of honor?"

Erwin rose. "I already gave you my word of honor. Why do you ask me twice?"

End of May, 1940

Erwin rolled over again and knew he would not fall back asleep. Even now, the lingering exhilaration of conquest woke him early each morning. In sitting up, he brushed a white envelope, which fell from his bed. He stooped, picked it up and opened it. Inside was a letter in German, handwritten in an archaic calligraphy.

> *You are masters of Holland for now, but powerful forces remain here, invisible to you. In this house lives a family beloved of many. Should any harm befall them, you personally will meet with the gravest consequences.*

Erwin hurried to his bedroom window and found the lock still secure. The letter's deliverer could only have entered through the hallway, from inside this house.

Who could have written this threat? A fledgling resister? A family friend? A lunatic? The writer clearly had no understanding of professional soldiers. As if the family were at any risk at all! But the defiant tone . . . and the fact that someone had placed the note on his bed . . . while he slept! Better not to show it; his men might be tempted to some kind of aggression, and that would only slow the recruiting. He placed the note in his private locker and carried his work papers to breakfast.

In the dining room Nagel served him two soft-boiled eggs in small silver *eierdoppen*. Erwin leafed distractedly through his papers, still thinking of the threatening note on his bed. Unable to focus on the papers, he broke the tops of the eggs with his tiny spoon and dipped moist German bread into the yolks. Across the hall he noticed the dark-haired mother helping the two children with their own breakfasts.

For weeks Erwin had barely noticed the mother in her gray skirts and white blouses, the thin pastel sweaters of orange and lavender. When Erwin crossed her path, he commented on the weather, or asked about the children without listening to the answer; that was all.

"A family beloved of many," the odd note had said. What had the family done to become so beloved?

"Tell us the Cunera legend," he heard the little girl say.

"Anna tells it better. And she tells you every time she sees you."

"We want to hear it from you."

"All right, I'll tell it, even though there are better stories."

The woman's stomach was tight as she leaned closer to the children; Erwin could imagine the perfect joining of her abdomen to her thighs. He turned away; nothing would be more ridiculous than to be caught seeming to stare at her.

The mother spoke in hushed, secret tones to the two children, and they listened with rapture to the story Erwin could not hear. When she finished, the mother and girl lifted the breakfast dishes. On an impulse, Erwin followed them into the kitchen, where they readied the tea tray he had seen before in Guse's room.

"You're kind to look after Lieutenant Guse."

She seemed to jump slightly at his voice.

"Sorry to startle you. I'll help you with the tray, if you don't mind."

The woman looked at him. "Do you take breakfast to all your wounded men?"

"He's the best of the unit I just trained." Erwin hesitated. "And my adopted son."

Now the woman looked into his eyes. "Your adopted son?"

"I was stationed near Kiel. My wife had recently died, two years after we married. No children." Erwin took a deep breath. "For a time, skating was my only pleasure. There's a kind of freedom, alone on the ice; maybe you know the feeling."

"Ready with the tray?" she asked.

He lifted and walked with her from the kitchen. "Anyway, at the skate-pond one day there was a group of teen-aged bullies. Germany was full of them after the War: boys with no future. They had caught a toddler and were sliding him across the ice to each other. Each time he came to a stop, the little boy struggled to get free. He didn't cry, but he had this earnest little face."

The woman paused and her pretty face flowered in sympathy. He was surprised how much the look meant to him, how much he suddenly wanted her to know his story.

"I scattered the bullies and carried the child into the village. I learned he was orphaned, under the care of the local church, so I adopted him." Erwin manufactured a laugh. "I never imagined that toddler growing into such a giant. He's an amazing young man, one of my best students."

Guse's room smelled of warm butter. Next to the bed, the woman's little son already sat in a chair, watching Guse. The woman

9

placed the tea tray on the bed stand. She cleared a breakfast tray and china dish with flecks of bread, smears of butter and boiled apples, drops of yolk and a ceramic *eierdop* with bits of eggshell. Erwin smiled at Guse, who smiled guiltily back.

June, 1940

Erwin jostled in the truck bed with his lieutenants, the wind blowing in their faces and flapping their sleeves. Nagel drove the truck east toward Wageningen, past the great dairy cows lying in pasture.

Werner Kessler spoke over the wind. "The locals say you can tell it's going to rain when the cows lie down!"

Dichter Strohn laughed. "It must be true! Every day the cows lie down, and every day it rains."

Erwin chuckled, his mind half-engaged in the lieutenants' chat, half on the mission. Recruiting and training Netherlanders would be something new. How much easier with a nucleus of his old students here to help.

"How's your Hollandish?"

"Better than yours!"

"Take it slowly," Erwin told them. "It's easy to sound foolish in someone else's language. Start in local language to show your good will, but move to German if necessary. They'll understand German if you speak slowly."

Over the truck rail they saw cardboard signs on stakes, with crude painted letters: "MOFFEN WEG!"

"What does it mean?"

"'Germans go home!' They call us *Moffen*!"

"Stop the truck," Erwin called to Nagel through the window. With the truck still rolling, Uwe Vogel and Wolfgang Zimmer leapt over the side, pulling up the signs and carrying them into the truck bed.

"Vandals!" Nagel called from the wheel. Erwin nodded to Nagel's reflection in the side mirror, and the truck accelerated again.

Kessler fingered the paint on one of the signs. "What a shame if no Netherlanders sign up."

"They might be the best, except maybe Scandinavians."

"Probably. The English call them 'the Dutch,' just like 'Deutsch!' Netherlanders are Germans, pretending they're not!"

Erwin shifted his weight on the wooden truck-bed. Who could predict? At Waterloo, Wellington counted Netherlanders his worst troops. But what might they do with the right training, the right leadership, the right cause?

Wolfgang Zimmer spoke with vigor through the wind. "They think we're fighting for Germany. How do you convince them they're fighting for Holland?"

Strohn said, "You'll fail if you think that way. It's not about Germany; it's much bigger."

Uwe Vogel shouted over the noise, "Just make the choices clear: if you don't like National Socialism, then it's capitalism or Russian communism!"

"Hucksters or Heroes!"

The truck stopped in Wageningen's market square. Leaping from the truck bed, the men unloaded boards, nails, paper and tools.

While he hammered, Zimmer asked, "But how can we make these choices clearer than they already are?"

Vogel answered as if no Netherlanders were near. "Good question! These people seem uninterested in the great issues."

"Maybe their defeat will make the issues real for them."

Erwin spoke over the lieutenants' hammering. "Never underestimate the call of Honor. The best will always want to test themselves, if only we can make the possibility clear."

He scanned their faces and offered a final caution. "That's the theme. Talk about the spiritual bleakness of capitalism. Talk about the chance to make history. Stay away from Plato, Kant and Hegel. I doubt these people even know who they are."

Strohn said, "The philosophical arguments persuaded me."

"I doubt that you're typical. For most people, speak to their hearts."

Erwin watched the recruiting station take final shape: a strange mix of *Wehrmacht Schrecklichkeit*, market-day trading booth, and university classroom. Pamphlets quoting Hegel and Kant and Hitler and Mussolini lay stacked on the booth counter.

It still surprised him no one chuckled at the posters: sneering Jews snatched the hard-won harvests of blond farmers; sinister shadows veiled a hammer and sickle; blond figures strode manfully over a shrunken Earth. Never mind. Others more skilled in propaganda had designed them, and they seemed to work, at least in Germany. He would learn the Hollandish reaction today.

To Nagel he gave a final instruction. "Prop up the invitations to the games; we want a lot of visitors. We'll have a little band like the one at Scheveningen Beach; I hear it's popular."

The booth was ready at last. The lieutenants spaced themselves around it, not to block or intimidate the shoppers threading past in ones and twos. How much time passed with no one stopping? It was awkward, in a way that recruiting in Germany never had been.

Eventually a tall Netherlander stopped. No surprise that he chose Kessler: the tall lieutenant had the kind of face that people instinctively approached, for directions or for help. The unsmiling Netherlander eyed a pamphlet wordlessly, then looked at Kessler. A few locals hovered as their evident leader began.

Erwin strained to hear as the Netherlander spoke. "You want to recruit Fascists?"

Answering the challenge, Werner Kessler, as tall as the Netherlander and broader-shouldered, held an even tone. "National Socialists."

"Why?" The Netherlander's companions made near-smiles and watched for Kessler's answer.

"It's the best system on Earth. So why wouldn't we?"

"What's good about it?"

"Well, for one thing, it works."

Careful, Erwin wished he could say to Kessler. Don't gloat. Emphasizing their battle humiliation would not win recruits.

Kessler spoke as if he knew Erwin's silent thoughts. "Let me ask you: what is virtue, in your eyes?"

The question seemed to irritate the Netherlander, wrong-footing him from his calm, prosecutorial tone. He nearly sneered as he answered. "Oh, telling the truth, keeping your promises, I suppose."

"What about self-sacrifice?"

"Self-sacrifice for what?"

"For your People."

The Netherlander smiled sarcastically. "How do you serve your People?"

"By obeying a leader who gives voice to its needs."

The Netherlander gave no expression.

Kessler went on. "We have a saying: *Gemeinnutz geht vor Eigennutz.*"

To Erwin's relief, the Netherlander nodded. "'Common good before private good.' I've heard it. I didn't know it was German."

Kessler said, "*Du bist nichts; dein Volk ist alles.*"

"'You are nothing; your people is everything'?" Translating, the Netherlander seemed to relax. Kessler had done well. Erwin stopped listening as their tone settled into genuine conversation.

Erwin moved his attention to Zimmer, facing a young farmer on the opposite side, his voice just audible: "Let me ask you: does democracy have any convictions? Genuine convictions, I mean, that people would stake their lives for?"

Of course the Netherlander could not answer; Erwin smiled privately.

"Can't you see the connection? German armies are winning everywhere; the democracies crumble like paper. Why?"

The young farmer nodded, as if absorbing the new thought. Well done, Erwin thought.

Erwin turned again to Strohn behind the booth, loading a young Netherlander with pamphlets.

Strohn said, "In my view, the choice is only this: either you choose to be a moral person or you do not."

No, no! Erwin wanted to throw his hat: exactly the kind of abstraction he wanted to avoid. Could he possibly have made it any clearer? On the other hand, maybe it was too much to ask. How could their unending discussion of philosophy not work its way into recruiting? But no one actually talks that way! Speak their language! Still, Erwin did not interrupt: a man Strohn's age had to be more effective than a forty-year-old colonel. His lieutenants showed what the recruits could become, and their demeanor spoke more truly than any words.

Erwin saw his forbearance rewarded as the Netherlander nodded, and Strohn's gaze roamed the man's face as he went on.

"And what can be more deeply moral than the surrender of self-interest for the benefit of the whole?"

"That's true, I guess."

Strohn was succeeding.

Erwin moved his attention again, and saw that even bird-faced, unsmiling Vogel had a lead. "Just look around. Do you know people with more money, better houses?"

Vogel's prospect nodded.

"Do they work harder? Are they more intelligent or more talented?"

The Netherlander shook his head. "No."

"Isn't it obvious your system doesn't reward virtue?"

Vogel, the clear-eyed pragmatist: appealing to logic, when the question was not a logical one at all, but spiritual. But Vogel surprised Erwin with his closing.

"Do you want to live in a society of money-lenders and shopkeepers, or a society of heroes?"

Vogel got three signatures over the next few hours. More, Erwin admitted, than even Guse might have gotten if he had healed enough to come.

PAARDENVELD
June, 1940

Sophia Vaubin van Dordrecht made her Saturday walk into Rhenen, her daughter Geertruide and her son Herbert each gripping her finger, Herbert skipping to keep up.

The tenant dairyman Bart van Oostveen walked with them, pushing a cart. Bart's pitchforking of the German lieutenant seemed only a strange dream, and Bart walked freely in the open air unchallenged. The dairyman was short and rail-thin, but strong; Sophia had seen him hoist a stricken ewe, fallen from the weight of her unshorn wool, and right her with no help. Among the invaders, Bart's company offered a feeling of security.

"Have you noticed people's expressions since the surrender?" Sophia asked. "Confused and sullen."

"The way a calf looks, just after he's castrated," Bart answered.

In town, Bart turned left and walked uphill toward the cooperative store. Sophia led the children to Market Street, looking for her oldest friends, Anna Meurs and Roosmarijn Poel, whom they called "Roos." In the square Sophia saw them together, gesturing as they spoke, turning to wave as they noticed Sophia, then hugging her with red happy faces.

"So glad to see you!" Sophia said. "Back in your houses?"

"Back in," Anna answered. "Maarten seems glad to see me."

"It was lucky Maarten didn't evacuate with you," Sophia answered. "Where else would I have found a doctor for the German lieutenant, after Bart pitchforked him?"

"Any bomb damage at Paardenveld?"

"No, our house was too far west of the fighting."

"Roos, did you?"

"Broken windows. That's all. Two blocks away, a house burned to the ground."

Herbert fidgeted. "I want to see Mr. Bloem."

"I'll meet you at his stall," Sophia answered.

Geertruide trotted away with Herbert.

Anna looked at Sophia, and asked, "Any word of Willem?"

Sophia answered, "He's not on any casualty lists. His father's still in Amsterdam trying to get word."

As if prompting Sophia, Anna said, "Sophia, you know Roos' brother died at Grebbeberg."

"He won the *Ridder M.W.O.* posthumously," Roos looked past them. "No sign on his grave."

"They're plain wooden crosses, aren't they?" Sophia asked soberly. "We should still go do something for it."

They were silent a minute, until Sophia remembered Roos' husband. "But Roos, what about Jan?"

"Nothing new. He fought at Grebbeberg, but he's not on any lists. We still hope he was captured, and coming back when the prisoners do."

"Jan and Willem, both," Sophia said. "Gone without a trace."

"Better missing than dead."

Anna looked them both squarely. "I almost feel guilty, with Maarten safe at home. Is there anything that he and I can do? Keep the children, cook a meal? Just say so."

"What's happening in Den Haag?" Roos asked.

"There's a *Reichsgoverner*, Seyss-Inquart," Anna answered. "An Austrian Nazi. They say he'll keep the old government in place, as long as it listens to him."

Sophia said, "He suspended the legislature on the 24th; I heard it on the radio."

"Be careful," Anna warned. "It's prison if you're caught with a radio on."

"They wouldn't." Roos glared.

"They already have. I heard of three Utrechters in jail already."

"Only for British radio: Radio *Oranje*."

"What else would you listen to?" Roos asked. "*Moffen* propaganda?"

Roos probed. "I still don't understand you, bringing Maarten to your house to treat a *Moff*. Why would you do that?"

"What if the Germans had found him dead on our property? And Roos, you should see him: he can't be twenty. You'd have done the same thing."

Before Sophia finished, Roos already blurted, "I'd have put him in a cart and thrown him in the woods."

"I treated him the way you'd want the Germans to treat Jan. The battle's over."

Roos scowled. "We'll fight again before we're free. Saving Nazis now only makes the job harder."

Anna began to speak of the weather, but Roos ignored her and asked Sophia, "How do you think your father-in-law will like having *Moffen* at Paardenveld?"

"I can't imagine. I considered writing them in Amsterdam, but I thought it might upset them less if I just tell them when they get home."

Anna made her peacemaking face. "Well, better shop before the stalls close down!"

Roos and Sophia forced cheerful replies.

"*Dag.*"

"*Tot ziens.*"

Sophia turned to catch up with the children. Each visit to Mr. Bloem's stall brought back those childhood Rotterdam Saturdays, when her father had taken Sophia for dockside strolls to see the great ships. The ships' steel sides rose high out of the water, dwarfing the tugboats: the massive black shining *Rotterdamsche Lloyd* ready to carry passengers to Aruba or Curacao or Batavia; the giant freighters alongside, still something about them of Africa, China, or Brazil. Her eyes had followed the mooring ropes thicker than a man's arm, running from the ship cleats through the chocks to the massive bollards on the harbor walls. Watching the stevedores handle the crates, her father said the freighters brought rubber, and tin, and cocoa, and coffee. Down the wharves they passed carts with carved toys from China, olives from the Mediterranean, strange fruits from Africa, intricate spice boxes from the Near East. Sophia the little girl could have stared a long time, wanting to know the names, the taste and use of each. But her father kept walking, blowing opaque white smoke from his cigar, and Sophia had followed.

After she married, Sophia had taken her father to Mr. Bloem's stall whenever he visited Rhenen. Her father always lingered and tasted samples, offering opinions on the quality and pondering the cause: weather, length of storage, a supplier's sagacity in choosing. When an item disappointed her father, he said so; any other reaction would have been disrespectful of Mr. Bloem's expertise. Mr. Bloem always agreed, shaking his head and explaining: the Congolese heat had bittered the cocoa; a broker had sold him less than his best.

When her father was not in town, Mr. Bloem gave Sophia samples to keep until her father came, to get his opinion. "Is your father Jewish?" Bloem had asked Sophia. "He's too much of a *mensch* to have no Jewish blood."

In 1938, esophagus cancer had found her father, shrinking him to a child's weight, feasting on his upper body, taking its cruel time like a gourmet. His choices were suicide, inexpressible pain, or morphine so strong it left him drooling and floundering on his bed. In the final, joyless weeks of her father's life, Sophia had begun to paint again: finding refuge in Spanish peaches against a mahogany cabinet; Egyptian pomegranates in a bowl of cold ceramic.

Now the wind blew twigs from Sophia's path as her shoes scuffed the cobbled street. She saw Mr. Bloem in his white shirt and black bow-tie, showing the children "Polish candies." The children begged her to buy some. She bought a handful, and Mr. Bloem smiled like a father at Sophia and crinkled his eyes.

Sophia took Bart and the children to meet Willem's parents at the station. Her in-laws stepped off the train from Amsterdam with their clothes still unwrinkled, but their faces more haggard than she had ever seen. Even their hellos to the children seemed strained. Sophia felt a sudden dread. "Still no news?"

Old Dr. van Dordrecht shook his head. "Nothing. Willem's not on any list."

Bart slung their luggage onto the little wicker cart.

There was no way to soften the news. Sophia said, "The Germans are organizing a training center at Paardenveld. The colonel has made the library his office, and he sleeps in the main bedroom."

Seeing her father-in-law's look of shock, Sophia added, "The colonel's behavior is very correct."

The old doctor was silent. His wife spoke scornfully. "Germans. They're dirty people."

The colonel was nowhere to be seen, sparing an awkward introduction. Sophia served everyone a small omelet and soup.

"I'll move us into the corner bedroom," her mother-in-law said.

Old Dr. van Dordrecht said nothing, and only poked at his food. "What's wrong?" his wife fussed. "You hardly ate your lunch, either."

"Too long away from home, I suppose. I've never felt so tired."

Someone was shaking Sophia. As Sophia woke, her mother-in-law's frightened face loomed close. "Sophia, come see. Something's wrong."

Sophia's stomach burned as she slung on a robe and followed Willem's mother to the corner bedroom. On the reading table a candle burned, and the clock showed 3:15. Dr. van Dordrecht lay on his side, eyes open, but his body motionless.

In turns the women waved their hands before his open eyes, which stayed inert.

Mrs. van Dordrecht let a tear fall. "He made a noise; it woke me up. I asked him if he'd had a nightmare, but he didn't answer."

"Stay with him," Sophia said to her. "I'll fetch Maarten."

Back in her room, Sophia tucked her nightgown into some old riding pants and buttoned on a sweater, hurried downstairs and pulled a lantern from the pantry. Starting the car would rouse the curfew police, so instead she fetched a bicycle from the shed.

Walking the bicycle out in the grayness, she recognized the colonel's adjutant Nagel, who seemed to spot her at the same time. "Is something wrong?"

Sophia kept her pace. "My father-in-law's sick; I'm fetching the doctor."

"How far?"

"Less than a kilometer."

"Why don't I take the motorcycle instead?" Nagel asked. "I can bring the doctor back in the sidecar."

"Let me give you a note," Sophia answered. "Otherwise you'll terrify him."

When Sophia returned with Maarten's note, Nagel already had the motorcycle running. The captain pocketed the note and scooted away.

Waiting for them, Sophia's mind wandered. Before the cancer, old Dr. van Dordrecht had become her father's good friend, asking about his import business, always inquisitive. The two fathers had walked Paardenveld together, discussing each new flowerbed or shrub. Willem was seldom part of these goings-on, or any other estate activities such as meeting the Farm Inspector. In fact, Willem had kept his distance from Paardenveld altogether. He saw patients for long hours at Sint Anna's Clinic. He never missed a university reunion, arriving home at the train station on Sunday evenings with Maarten. He joined Maarten for half-day bicycle tours through the countryside, like a *jonkheer* of four hundred years ago inspecting his fief. Old Dr. van Dordrecht once wondered aloud how a man with such a perfect wife could stay away so often.

The motorcycle's rip called back Sophia's thoughts. Through the half-light she saw Maarten's tall frame angled crazily up from the low sidecar. The engine stopped, and Maarten's long body extracted itself; his hands clasped Sophia's with a friend's reassurance before he hurried after her upstairs.

In the bedroom, Maarten's examination was brief. "Almost certainly a stroke. We should move him to Sint Anna's."

Old Mrs. van Dordrecht asked, "What will happen?"

"He could stop breathing any minute, or he could be like this for some time." Maarten stopped. "Sophia, what is it?"

Sophia had been the first to notice Dr. van Dordrecht's new stillness. She put her hand over his mouth and nose. "Come see."

Maarten checked for breathing again, then felt the pulse. "He's dead," Maarten told them.

Dr. van Dordrecht's eyes were still open.

Under clouds that seemed barely a hundred meters aloft, Erwin watched the long sad line inch past the receiving family. In black, Sophia Vaubin van Dordrecht and her mother-in-law greeted neighbors, and took earnest kisses on the cheek from white-haired aristocrats just arrived from the western cities, who recognized each other in line and waved briefly. Wind bursts flapped the men's pant legs; the women needed both hands to hold their dresses down.

The mourners' glances at Erwin were cold. He stood apart, wishing at least to show respect. Erwin had never seen a funeral so large, a mark of the World's esteem for Dr. van Dordrecht. Till now, Erwin had never imagined his own funeral; but today he knew that his should be like this.

Guse, walking again, towered over Bart the dairyman; an onlooker might never guess that one had nearly killed the other. Both stayed close to Sophia van Dordrecht, ready to run little errands, but never did Erwin see her accept Guse's help. She did not even acknowledge his presence by sending him away.

Nagel hovered about, an uninvited butler. Erwin's lieutenants strolled the lawns, offering extra umbrellas against the tangible mist, taking a chair to an old guest. Some accepted these favors. Others only looked away.

At the coffin's lowering, on Erwin's command, his lieutenants raised single-bolt rifles and fired in unison; after all, Dr. van Dordrecht was a retired colonel. His lieutenants saluted the grave in the style of Hollanders, with palms facing down.

Erwin watched the mourners, hoping they recognized his gestures of respect, and sensed his good intentions.

Erwin and his officers lingered after the visitors broke away, until at last Sophia van Dordrecht approached him. "You seemed moved by the funeral."

Erwin was surprised she had noticed him; he had never seen any indication she knew he was there. He recovered quickly. "A man with so many to mourn his passing. From what I can tell, he was a man I would have respected very much."

"Did it occur to you that taking his house may have caused his stroke?"

Her directness surprised him; but reflexively he met it in kind. "Speaking very frankly, yes. It's regrettable."

"Regrettable?"

Erwin faltered; was the emotion comprehensible to someone with no combat experience? "It might surprise you: a soldier often feels his adversary's suffering, just as Achilles and Priam could admire each other and know each other's pain. But they also knew the gods had set them at odds, irreconcilably. That's how History moves us now. I can see little tragedies, but I don't waver."

He looked for her reaction, but she changed the subject. "Excuse me; I have to meet the Farm Inspector. Willem's father used to handle these meetings."

Erwin watched her cross the lawn and greet the most ordinary man he had ever seen; if asked to describe the Farm Inspector later, he would have struggled. The Farm Inspector. What could life be like for such a being? Surely the meeting was a great inconvenience, but look at her: so polite to this pest! The next time he saw her alone, Erwin would offer to warn this bumpkin away.

CELEBRATION
July, 1940

"Colonel, you look like a man about to see his father."

Erwin looked up from his desk. "What do you mean?"

"Happy, that's all."

Nagel's familiarity! Erwin scratched a note to mention it later, when he could take the right tone. For now he just asked, "What time does General Langer arrive?"

"Ten o'clock. I'll bring in lunch at noon." Nagel finished straightening things and disappeared.

Erwin was at the great hall window when the Mercedes tires crunched the gravel in front. Out of the staff car stepped a thinning old man. Through General Langer's scarce white hair, and his aging skin that no longer reflected the light, Erwin still saw the man of twenty years earlier: the man who had sheltered him when the *Wehrmacht* was dismantling, who hiked with him tirelessly in the South German hills, who introduced him to the spirituality of Nature. In those days, General Langer had looked the way Erwin looked now: prize-winning fencer and glittering with medals.

Nagel saluted and helped Langer's adjutant, Captain Sinder, with the luggage. Just in front of the massive front door, Erwin extended a hand and General Langer reddened with pleasure.

"Well, Erwin, how do you like your headquarters?"

Erwin chuckled. "*Gezellig*, as the locals say. I'm getting a lot done."

"Guse's recovered?"

"Walking, but limited. Spoiled rotten by the woman who lives here."

Erwin closed the heavy door and led General Langer over the black-and-white marble floor, the floor still smelling of Nagel's ammonia.

"How are Strohn, and Kessler, and Zimmer, and Vogel?"

"Anxious to see you."

General Langer grinned. "Splendid! I have medals for each of them."

They entered the library. The General's gaze roamed with an amused smile until Erwin gestured to a chair. Erwin felt odd to sit at his own desk with his superior sitting across like a subordinate, but General Langer quickly broke the ice. "Did you see the latest edition of *Signal?*" he asked. "With the photograph of Hitler strolling down the *Champs Elysees?*"

"I saw," Erwin answered. "With Goering and Rommel and Borman!"

The General was right: nothing better captured the *Zeitgeist* unfolding this summer than the image of Hitler in Paris.

Their eyes played happily in the silence. General Langer smiled quizzically. "You don't mind losing your tanks, and becoming a teacher again?"

"Let Rommel keep the tanks," Erwin replied. "I'd be happier if we fought with swords. I am looking forward to teaching again. Prototyping an elite corps of Aryans from another country, with the Myrmidons helping, that's exciting."

General Langer grinned again. "The Myrmidons! I didn't realize you knew your group's nickname. I'd have thought anyone was afraid to say it in front of you."

"The Myrmidons? I can't remember who told me, I think Colonel Schussler. I took it as a compliment: it can only mean I'm Achilles." Erwin looked at the General. "Perhaps I'm naive; you've always sheltered me from *Wehrmacht* politics."

"Hitler himself would shelter you. In Poland no commanders kept pace with you or Colonel Schussler."

That was General Langer's way of putting things; no one made Erwin feel more like a hero.

"Well, I've handled my work free of political pressures," Erwin said. "Thanks to you, I'm sure. Anyway, what news from Colonel Schussler?"

"He's been doing in Poland what you begin here, with success, I think." General Langer smiled. "Horst Schussler: my other great protégé; Erwin Schell's only rival."

"My only friend," Erwin answered. "Except you."

General Langer studied the bookshelves and the giant window panes. "The medals ceremony should make a good impression."

"I agree. I've also advertised sports competitions for tomorrow, open to the new recruits, even other Netherlanders who haven't joined yet. If you can stay for it, the Myrmidons should excel; this will show the recruits what they can become."

"Wonderful. I'll tell Sinder I'm staying an extra day."

Already Erwin felt satisfaction, watching the Hollandish volunteers forming on the lawn. Sophia van Dordrecht stood on the side with her children; her mother-in-law must have refused to come out.

In his clear, elegant voice, General Langer called each lieutenant to be honored.

"Werner Kessler."

Erwin knew muscular Kessler's story nearly as well as Guse's, his own sons; Erwin could actually see the world through Kessler's eyes. As a boy in Koblenz, Kessler had watched the flowing Rhine, and imagined its course through Cologne and Dusseldorf, to where it veered west to Rotterdam and finally mingled into the North Sea, where vessels began their way about the broad World: to old Hanseatic ports northward; to the Mediterranean; to exotic Brazil; to unimaginable China. Kessler had built model ships, and dreamed of their passages. He had studied the ocean currents, the seafloor's contours, the marine chemistry giving rise to life. Sea-loving Kessler came of age too late to join the Kaiser's great surface fleet, scuttled at Scapa Flow after the Great War. And Kessler had no love for U-boat life, long weeks in cramped spaces under the ocean. Erwin had found him just in time to steer him into his elite group of dry-land warriors.

Kessler doubled his chin looking down at the *Ritter Kreuz* General Langer pinned to his tunic.

"Wolfgang Zimmer."

Erwin knew Zimmer's story too, as if he'd written it. Zimmer had apprenticed at the famous Dortmunder Brewery, his father the chief chemist for a barley-malter. The Doemens Braumeister School had accepted him just weeks before the Munich Accord. Much Zimmer already knew: storage of hops, malt and yeast, mixing and boiling, yeast pitching, fermentation, filtration, casking and conditioning. At the Doemens school, the knowledge would become systematic, and he would learn the dry Czech Pilseners, the malty Helles of Munich, and the Vienna lagers, maltier still. He would learn the famous Marzen beers, the Dunkels, the Hefe Weizens, the Bocks and Weizenbocks.

The brewery had been a kind of refuge. Away from it, Zimmer had been exposed to a meanness, a recklessness he could not name: sado-masochism on street-corner posters; angry manifestos of radical groups, spitting with hatred against the Weimar republican government.

Zimmer's father, with his thin white hair in full retreat on his balding head, seemed also in full retreat from the malaise everywhere. Herr Zimmer worked long hours. At home, he only rested to restore his energy for more work; brewing must have been the only topic he ever discussed with his son.

Wolfgang's older brother Hans had retreated into a *wandervogel* that roamed the land purposelessly, singing folk songs, making no sense when he visited.

When Erwin had found Zimmer at a Dortmund recruiting station, they spoke for more than an hour. Erwin knew what Zimmer saw in him, his new mentor: an alternative to the pornography, the radicals' destructive rage, the *wander* clubs' dreaminess. Erwin offered heroism, in the Fatherland's service. At the induction ceremony, Zimmer's father had seemed relieved.

Now Zimmer's eyes scanned the Hollandish recruits, the other Myrmidons, and Sophia van Dordrecht as he received the medal and shook General Langer's hand.

"Dichter Strohn."

Erwin stifled a smile. His philosopher-student came from Melle, northeast of Dortmund. Strohn's father had been "King" of the village shooting club, Melle's greatest social honor, winning the kingship in the annual shooting contest. Afterward, that year and all others, Herr Strohn joined his club friends in drinking the *Haltsfeller*: cold vodka with a sunken salami and horseradish.

His mother must have chosen Dichter's name. And surely the unmasculine name only pressured him to equal his father. When Erwin's recruiters came to Melle, Strohn had joined at once; the father and everyone else burned with pride as soon as they heard.

"Knight's Cross, First Class."

"Uwe Vogel."

Vogel was Erwin's favorite, second only to Guse. Of them all, Vogel was plainest in manner, visibly restless making small talk, just like Erwin as a young man. Vogel took instruction well. He was the purest among them in absence of vanity.

Vogel's Pomeranian father had struggled to earn a grocer's living in the desperate years. When Uwe visited his married sister in Berlin, he had chanced across Erwin's recruiter. His father had raised no objection; at home the future looked bleak.

Erwin's mind wandered again and he scanned the crowd. A mild drizzle began.

"Reinhard Guse."

Erwin's looked up at his son, standing a head taller than the others. He read Guse's mind: visibly pleased to see Sophia van Dordrecht standing just behind the little crowd.

"Knight's Cross, First Class."

The next morning's silver fog had already burned off when Anna and Maarten arrived. Sophia was glad they were joining her to watch the German games.

"There were signs all over town," Maarten laughed. He unfolded a cheap poster ad. "'Beer! Music! Demonstrations! Sports!' Only Germans can make a picnic sound like work."

"They're trying hard," Anna said.

A little brass band played in the nearest pasture. Two hired waiters served beer.

Anna's mild face frowned. "Roos wouldn't come."

"She thinks watching the Germans means supporting them," Sophia answered. "Willem's mother won't come out, either."

Maarten gestured toward the men in new uniforms. "Those are the recruits?"

"They are. Yesterday was the first time I'd seen them here as a group."

"They look so severe. Are they trying to act like Germans?"

"Or how they imagine Germans act!"

"They certainly look like farmers," Sophia said. "Men Bart would feel at home with."

"Men Bart probably knows."

"Has Bart said anything about joining?"

"Of course not."

Maarten looked at his paper flyer. "Tug-of-war, races, boxing, wrestling, fencing, rifle- and pistol-shooting: these are propaganda games, to make the Germans look good."

He handed Anna the paper. "What about skating?" He glanced around before he continued in a low voice. "With skating I'd change their mind about who's the Master Race."

The women half-smiled. "It would be hard to organize skating in July."

"Then remind the Colonel this winter."

"I think they chose sports they consider heroic," Sophia said. "See the swords they wear? They look ridiculous, don't they? But they practice with them constantly! And they talk about the characters in the *Iliad* as if they were real people."

"An odd bunch, aren't they?"

Sophia made a mischievous face. "Would you like to meet the Colonel? Now's your chance, while they're trying to make friends!"

"No, thanks."

Tight over the ground, the Myrmidons staked a canvas square for wrestling, boxing and fencing.

"I like the look of your recruits," General Langer told Erwin.

"Look how many spectators today, more than I expected."

"I wonder what they're thinking. Here to learn, or to mock us?"

"Either way, let's hope the games make an impression."

"Let's hope. What's Guse doing today?"

"Just pistol and rifle. He's still weeks away from full recovery. It's a shame; he'd win the wrestling and boxing."

"Well, the others must be glad of a chance." General Langer studied the sky. "So far still clear. What are the chances of good weather all day?"

"Oh, you can be sure of some drizzle at some point. But I'm starting to think like the locals. They just ignore it unless it's pouring rain."

The wrestlers unbuttoned their shirts and pulled them off.

"Look," Erwin said. "Look how they smile at Guse!"

General Langer chuckled. "They're embarrassed to compete for his crown with him watching."

"Look how he grins back. He knows what they're thinking."

Shirtless in the sunlight, Zimmer and Kessler gleamed with sweat as they struggled for the championship, each fending off the other from gripping his belt, shoving, staggering, recovering before the other could take advantage. Zimmer's knee hit the canvas first. His other leg pushed to turn away before Kessler could grip him from behind, but too late: Kessler's arms snaked under Zimmer's, and his hands locked over Zimmer's neck.

"Enough!" Nagel refereed. "Save some strength for the boxing!"

Kessler let go. They rose and shook hands, their chests heaving.

The breeze fluttered the paper targets; each shooter waited for a stillness, let his breath go out and squeezed. Each shot cracked the still air, and the biting smell of the gunpowder wafted to the onlookers.

Erwin saw the boy Herbert standing too close, almost at the firing line, and stepped to move him back, but Guse left the contestants and reached the boy first. Guse hoisted the boy on his shoulders until the boy laughed.

Strohn's last shot hit the black circle in dead center. Vogel's shot landed just enough right to perceive the difference. Guse's struck only a pinhead further out.

"Vogel and Strohn always compete for first in shooting," Erwin told General Langer.

"What next?" Langer asked.

"A short break, I think. In fifteen minutes, the qualifying sprints."

At the sprint track, the onlookers already there made way as Erwin and General Langer approached. On the opposite side, Erwin saw Sophia van Dordrecht with a pretty blond friend, and a ridiculous tall man wearing the thickest glasses he had ever seen, the three chatting quietly and only half watching.

Ten paces off the gun, Strohn and Vogel separated from the others. They ran as if chained together, not a speck of air between them over the first ninety meters. Then, over the last ten meters it seemed an unseen chair lifted Strohn up and forward; even his arms seemed out of stride with the finishing speed of his legs.

Erwin called to them softly at the finish line. "Well done, both of you."

He turned to General Langer. "Something to drink?"

"No, thank you. I'll wait until afterward."

They strolled to the canvas square and chatted distractedly through the early boxing rounds, until the final match between Zimmer and Kessler. Erwin noticed the low, gathering clouds and hoped for one more hour without rain.

"Oh!" the crowd shuddered spontaneously as Zimmer drew first blood from Kessler, with a cross-cut right that landed too far forward on Kessler's face to knock him down, but caught the tender part of his nose and upper lip against the turn of his head. Tiny spatters of blood flew all the way into the little crowd. A flash of anger marred Kessler's face; he ducked his head and stepped into Zimmer, but Zimmer stopped his rush with two tidy punches.

"Stop!" Nagel shouted. "Enough for today! One championship for each of you."

Zimmer handed Kessler a towel, who dabbed it against his nose and lip as the blood still ran. The skin around Kessler's mouth was pink and swelling.

"You've never punched like that before," Kessler said through the towel.

"I thought I was fighting for survival," Zimmer answered. "You should have seen how you looked, coming at me after my first punch."

General Langer smiled at Erwin. "What next?"

"The three-kilometer run starts soon. Vogel will win, unless one of the recruits surprises me."

They hurried to watch the runners assemble on the river road. Kessler and Zimmer sat out; Strohn and Vogel were surrounded by recruits in shorts.

Vogel shook Strohn's hand. "Hope you're not too tired from the sprints to give me your best race."

Strohn heaved out a laugh, high-strung with anticipation. "Don't use your psychology on me!"

Vogel gave a look of surprise, then laughed and patted Strohn's back.

The two Germans disappeared first, out of sight on the river road heading west toward Elst. The slowest recruits were still in view as Erwin, Nagel and General Langer ambled to Paardenveld's eastern edge to wait for the leaders, looking northward on the Veenendaal road.

Vogel's smaller frame appeared. Strohn showed two seconds later, the only challenger.

"Strohn looks more determined," Nagel said.

"That's how I know he'll lose," Erwin replied. "Vogel's stride is effortless, so natural: watch."

It seemed Vogel and Strohn ran at the same speed, even as the gap between them spread. Vogel finished twenty meters ahead, put his hands on his hips and walked toward the dike to recover, chest heaving, shoulders high and eyes on the ground, then slowed to let Strohn catch him. They shook hands without looking up, then walked together toward the dike.

"They'll need a few minutes before the tug-of-war," Erwin said to General Langer.

"Where will that be?"

"Behind the canal in the pasture."

In the tug-of-war championship, both teams tore the pasture with their boots, each man kicking to find purchase, flexing hard, then giving slightly as the acid in his legs forced him to rely for a moment on his teammates.

For ten minutes they pulled evenly, but once Zimmer's team faltered, they failed utterly, and Kessler's group pulled them past the divider like children. The losers staggered to regain their balance, then shook hands heavily with the winners.

"Time at last for the fencing," General Langer smiled at Erwin. "I assume you'll enter?"

"I shouldn't, since I'm the teacher. But I get so few chances."

Erwin tried to ignore the watchers as his soles scraped the canvas. His calves and ankles showed their old limberness and he celebrated the feel of his footwork and balance. He knew each Myrmidon, and how much effort to give each contender. Each challenger did his best, and Erwin could measure, even as he labored, the skills he had cultivated in each one. Strohn was last and closest to Erwin's level; the teacher held very little back against this emerging student. But Strohn had not surpassed Erwin yet. As judge, General Langer, discriminating against Erwin for his expertise, still had to smile and acknowledge Erwin's superiority.

Fencing always brought a mild elation. Out of breath, Erwin approached the beer table near Sophia van Dordrecht. Erwin glanced at her; for a moment he imagined she wanted to begin a conversation.

Instead she only smiled. "Congratulations, Colonel." When she finally spoke, her offhand tone almost mocked him, as if he had just won at a children's game. It jarred him somehow to realize the virtuosity he had just displayed on the fencing canvas was invisible to her.

Still breathing hard from his effort, Erwin fumbled for something offhand to say in answer. She walked away before he began.

"You spoke to him?" Anna asked.

"Only congratulations," Sophia told her. "But you know what I was thinking?"

"What?

"At the beer table, he was breathing so hard, I'm sure very proud of his fencing and expecting me to say something about it." Sophia thought of the pink skin pulsing tight and vulnerable against the colonel's windpipe. "Those ridiculous blades they carry: do they ever imagine one at their own neck? They live in a fantasy, as if there's no connection to reality."

Maarten interrupted as he rejoined them. "Well, I drank their beer and didn't enlist. I guess that's a small victory."

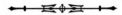

Erwin gave a little dinner for the Myrmidons and General Langer. So near the solstice, full day lit the back garden past nine o'clock; afterward the sun still lingered at the horizon, leaving a dusky light. From brown bottles Nagel filled their beer glasses.

General Langer looked over his beer glass at Erwin. "You're off to a good start with this group."

"Thank you."

"This is more important than any combat you could lead right now. If you succeed, Scandinavians may follow. Eventually the English."

Erwin wanted General Langer to hear how he spoke to the lieutenants. "You understand," he told them. "These recruits need you as mentors. Their success is your responsibility."

Nagel served a pork tenderloin, braised for hours, on a bed of stewed sauerkraut with tiny skinned potatoes. From a green bottle glistening with condensation, he poured a pale Moselle into their wine glasses. General Langer raised his wine glass, and looked from man to man. "To Beauty."

The toast might have been laughable coming from anyone they respected less.

"To Beauty." All the lieutenants replied with the same reverence they used in answering Erwin's own toasts, always "to Honor."

Erwin knew General Langer enjoyed the presence of these men, knew that Langer considered Erwin's success his own. But tonight General Langer showed more than his usual pleasure.

"The Rhineland. Austria. Czechoslovakia." The General tilted his wine glass each time he named a country. "Poland. Norway. Denmark. Holland. Belgium. Now France. This *Wehrmacht* amazes even its leaders."

Erwin listened happily.

"Hitler saw it, before anyone, how unready they all were."

"Especially in Poland," Erwin agreed. "Cavalry on horseback, with nothing but lances!" Erwin waved his fork as he spoke. "Holding formation and advancing to meet my tanks. An unbelievable slaughter of brave Polish soldiers."

General Langer said, "Everyone else laughs about those Polish lancers."

"The timid English and French gave no help. That silly cavalry was all the Poles had. The way they charged, no hesitation --" Erwin shook his head and looked down, as if talking to himself -- "what a sense of honor!"

General Langer said, "And Hitler was shrewd to take one opponent at a time."

Erwin nodded, listening happily again.

"The English know fighting is pointless. She can do more as a partner than as a defeated wasteland."

Erwin frowned. "What about Churchill?"

"Parliament doesn't really support him, not even his own party. No Tories think England can withstand our attack."

"I can see why. Their army hasn't shown any great ability."

"In August, more than a thousand planes will cross the Channel and destroy England's air force. Once we control the skies, English warships must leave the Channel, and our troops will cross. In a ground war the *Wehrmacht* could not lose."

General Langer looked at them as if letting them in on a secret. "With England quiet, we can have the final reckoning with the Bolsheviks. Then even England will applaud."

THREE SEASONS
July, 1940

Erwin's voice floated in the misty air. The sun hung just off the horizon.

"You ride with Charles Martel at Tours. If you lose, Europe becomes a Muslim province.

"You carry a musket at Waterloo. If Napoleon wins, the Netherlands becomes French for hundreds of years.

"Every important decision in history was made on the battlefield."

There was so much he could say. The trick was to know what to leave out.

"For thousands of years my country has been surrounded by invaders. This adversity made us strong. Think of your own country's struggles against Spain, England, France. Maybe your history has given you strength, too."

He watched for a reaction, but the recruits showed none.

"What keeps a people of such strength from leading the world?"

He paused. "The answer must be that we've chosen not to lead. Today I'm asking you to choose the opposite. Today I invite you to become an agent of History."

Erwin began to feel the connection with the recruits, as if electric current ran from him to each and back.

"Consider our *Führer's* words:

> *However weak the individual may be when compared with the omnipotence and will of Providence, yet at the moment when he acts as Providence would have him act he becomes immeasurably strong.*

He went on. "A small band of Heroes, acting as a group, can change civilization. But only with preparation. Look around at the men training you."

The lieutenants Guse, Kessler, Zimmer, Vogel and Strohn traded glances.

"They're all expert in hand-to-hand fighting, in riflery, even in tank warfare. Training with them, you'll develop the skills of professionals. But real strength lies not in the single man, but in the fighting unit. Over time you'll think as a group, which makes you strong, the way a thread becomes stronger, woven into fabric. That's what I'm watching for."

He glanced around the assembled rows a final time. "That is all."

His new men talked excitedly. He could not resist the temptation to listen, straining to translate. One little group spoke of England, then of Russia, then:

"Who's that black-haired woman?"

"They say her husband's away! Maybe she's available."

"She'll be available if I find her alone!"

Before the sound of the last word faded, Erwin reached the man and slapped his face twice, so hard that blood trickled from the nose. Erwin spat his words: "What do you think this is?"

The man was too shocked to answer.

"Didn't you hear a word I spoke? You think we're recruiting thugs to molest women?"

He shoved the stunned man. "Am I wrong? Answer me!"

Erwin's voice went cold. "Turn in your uniform to Captain Nagel and be gone in thirty minutes." Erwin gripped the haft of his sword and said, "If I ever see you near that woman, you won't see this sword in its sheath, but swinging. Understand?"

With sunken shoulders the man plodded toward Nagel.

Suddenly Erwin noticed the faces of the other recruits and realized he had shocked them. He stopped and looked the nearest ones in the eye. "We fight to save Civilization. Not to destroy it."

That night Erwin hardly slept; it was a relief when morning came. Under the overcast morning sky he carried mail to the oak table and sipped the hot coffee Nagel brought.

Sophia Vaubin van Dordrecht's voice broke the silence. Through the shrubbery leaves Erwin saw her kneel with the children, and she pointed at the near clouds. "Look, Geertruide; look, Herbert: Holland's the Land of the Low Sky. The clouds are so low because God in Heaven wants to be near us all."

Herbert and Geertruide looked solemnly at her, then at the clouds, then nodded. She rose again and led them around the garden until suddenly her eyes caught Erwin's.

"*Herr Kolonel*," she began in German.

"Yes?" Erwin answered.

"Each Sunday we say a vespers in the chapel. We start at eight o'clock and stay about forty-five minutes. It would mean a lot not to be disturbed; it's a way of keeping a family hour sacred. You can imagine this is a difficult time."

Why did she only ask now, after so many weeks? She must have been afraid before. Erwin tried to make a reassuring face. "Don't worry. You won't be disturbed."

In Rhenen's ancient Cunerakerk, Sophia sat between the children on a hardwood pew, vibrating with the organ chords. Her eyes strayed to the great organ pipes behind the choir, ranged from tiny flutes to great bassettes. Herbert fidgeted, and she squeezed his hand.

Sophia believed almost nothing in the Christian Bible. She knew that something had set in motion the phenomena that led to life, and she considered the gift of life a kind of miracle, a miracle that took the image of a Creator. This Creator's image sustained her. Though fatherless for some unknowable period, their nation occupied, her children still owned the Creator's blessed gift. Singing and praying in the Cunerakerk revived her mindfulness of this Creator and the Creator's precious gift. She scanned her fellow worshipers, each one a product of the same miracle, and felt a kind of communion.

Afterward she lingered with the children to drink tea with the congregation outside, before they strolled away and out of the city.

On the river road they passed the recruits. Fully recovered, the German lieutenant Guse gave a pistol demonstration, hitting small targets on the dike. Herbert stopped and stared, transfixed. Lieutenant Guse noticed the boy and returned his gaze until Sophia scooped Herbert up.

That afternoon, through the back window Sophia saw the lieutenant kicking a ball with Herbert. Each time she came to the window and looked, Guse and Herbert still kicked and ran. The German's face showed such pleasure that Sophia could imagine him as the orphan Erwin had described: the abandoned toddler who might have been glad to have Herbert as a friend. On and off for an hour she watched unseen, letting them play before she finally called Herbert inside.

Sophia closed the heavy chapel door and listened for any sound that might pass through. Hearing none, she locked it. Geertruide and Herbert sat on either side of their grandmother. The sight of them, the remains of her family, soothed an anxiety Sophia had not realized she felt.

Her bond with her mother-in-law had taken time. On their first meeting, Sophia had felt Mrs. Vaubin van Dordrecht's discomfort; imagined the type of bride that Willem's mother would have called a "better match": blondish, more extroverted, less foreign-looking. A Roos. But the doubts had visibly dissolved, as the grandmother had watched Sophia raising the children. Only weeks before the invasion, Willem had joked that the old woman was fonder of Sophia than of him.

By the altar Sophia knelt, and took each child's hand. "I have always told you to respect the truth. But when there's no freedom, honest people have to lie."

She uncovered a radio from the long cabinet. "You must never tell anyone about this. If anyone ever asks, even Anna or Roos, even Bart, it does not exist. Do you understand me? Geertruide?"

"I understand."

"Herbert?"

"Yes, mamma."

Sophia raised the radio's volume just enough to hear through the crackling static, glancing back to the door and wondering if any sound filtered through.

They listened to five minutes of English broadcasting. Then the Dutch-language program Radio *Oranje* began, and Sophia felt a new warmth. She heard news of the submarine war, and of the fighting in Africa.

Then her mother-in-law's eyes brightened at the sound of the Queen Wilhelmina's voice, recognizable over the airwaves. Old Mrs. Van Dordrecht, whose own father and husband had been *jonkheren*, knew the Queen personally. Over the radio Queen Wilhelmina said it was certain the Germans would be thrown out. She did not explain how. The children strained their faces, watching for Sophia's reaction.

Next came a string of farmer sayings, in nonsensical sequence:

"High trees catch much wind."

"After the calf is drowned, men fill the pond."

"With unwilling dogs, it's poor rabbit hunting."

"We must row with the oars that we have."

Code language for resisters, listening in attics, Sophia imagined.

Then the broadcast switched oddly to Spanish:

Senora Vaubin, Senora Vaubin.

Sophia stood transfixed.

El tio no esta infermo. El tio no esta infermo.

The speaker accented his "no."

It was unbelievable. But as to its meaning, she had no doubt. Sophia looked at her mother-in-law through tears that surprised her.

"What is it, Sophia?"

"You knew Willem and I met in Spanish class?"

The old woman nodded and smiled.

Sophia continued. "He used to joke about the silly beginners' phrases. '*Mi tio esta infermo*: my uncle is sick.'"

Willem's mother nodded again, still smiling. Now Sophia lowered her voice, nearly whispering. "The announcer said, '*Senora Vaubin. Senora Vaubin. El tio no esta infermo.*' The uncle's not sick."

She watched her mother-in-law's expression. Seeing none, Sophia said, "Willem must have asked them to say that for me! He must be in England!"

Willem's mother smiled uncertainly. "Why isn't Willem in school?"

The question stunned Sophia. Was her mother-in-law going addled, so soon after her husband's death? Sophia realized that her own shock must have shown, as she saw her mother-in-law recoil in alarm. Now Sophia looked at the door again. The program had ended; she was wasting dangerous time in the chapel. She bit her lip, turned off the set and closed it in the long cabinet.

She stroked her mother-in-law's arm. "Let's go to bed. We can talk tomorrow."

Upstairs Sophia helped Herbert with his pajamas and told a story. In her own room, she wondered about Willem's mother.

Sophia slept uneasily until she dreamed she had answered Willem's radio message, and that Willem had come home.

August, 1940

"Sophia! Why do you read the Nazi Party newspaper?" Roos' tone was like a mother to a naughty child.

"Did you know the air battle over Britain has started?" Sophia asked.

Sophia handed Roos the August 14 *Folk and Fatherland*, with its giant headline: ***DAY OF THE EAGLE!***

Roos read aloud in mock-dramatic:

> *Yesterday fifteen hundred planes attacked British airfields. All of southeast England is smoldering. British planes fall like rain, for only a few German losses.*

"How ridiculous!" Roosmarjin said. "Cartoon language."

Every day that month, Sophia bought the paper alone and carried it home. Each day she read of lop-sided British airplane losses, new proof that the island was bombed into stupor, new forecasts of English surrender.

Sunday in the chapel, Radio *Oranje* replayed a Churchill speech. The English Prime Minister's joy and relief vibrated through the radio.

> *The gratitude of every home in our island, in our Empire, and indeed throughout the world, except in the abodes of the guilty, goes out to the British airmen who, undaunted by odds, unwearied in their constant challenge and mortal danger, are turning the tide of war by their prowess and by their devotion . . . Never in the field of human conflict was so much owed by so many to so few.*

It was Churchill's tone that convinced her: the Germans were losing. No wonder the *Reichsgovernor* Seyss-Inquart made it a crime to listen to British broadcasting.

November, 1940

Anna sat with Maarten on the overstuffed love seat. Jan and Roos crowded round the low table with their red-faced children, just in from football on the lawn: thirteen-year-old Bernhard, nine-year-old Cornelia, and five-year-old Michiel. Roos still blushed with happiness and relief from Jan's surprise return from the German prison. For the first time since the May Days, everyone was at Paardenveld. Everyone but Willem.

Sophia poured steaming black coffee into porcelain cups and passed a dish of *koekjes,* two for each guest, although it was rude to take more than one. Jan took two and nobody cared; it was wonderful to see him out of prison camp, taking too many *koekjes.*

"Tell us the whole story, Jan."

"Oh," he looked away. "You don't want to hear it."

Maarten leaned forward, earnestly. "Tell us."

"Where do I start? The German tanks were running wild south of the rivers. But we controlled the bridges, which meant that Holland could last until the English and the French came. As long as my regiment held the Germans east of the Grebbe line."

Jan looked at Sophia. "Have you got some paper? I'll draw it.

Jan sketched quickly and pointed. "Here. First were the front screens, nothing more than a line of trenches. Four hundred meters back, our main line ran north along the Grift's west bank. Just behind it, all over the hill's eastern slope were our little porcupines, with steel domes and machine guns. Several hundred meters back, where the hill flattens out, we had troops in a stop-line.

"We knew they'd try to cross at the bridge over the Grift. To stop them we had the horn-work." He drew star-shaped hills with bunkers facing east and covering each other. "My group covered the horn-work and bridge from just behind" – Jan pointed to his drawing – "there. If the horn-work fell, we were supposed to detonate the bridge."

Jan looked through the window. "It's so odd, telling the story with Germans just outside."

"They'll go soon," Sophia answered. "They always stay after drills with the recruits, but never long."

Jan lowered his gaze and sipped his coffee. "We thought the Germans would take days to clear the skirmish lines farther east, and reach our screens. We had cut trees on the approaches, but we hadn't finished clearing them in time." He laughed bitterly. "The felled trees actually gave the Germans better cover."

Jan looked at Sophia. "You know the house where the Wageningen road meets the Cuneraweg? I forget the owner's name, the man who owns the brick factory upstream."

"The one who joined the Nazi party before the invasion?"

"Right, the NSB man. We evacuated his house with everyone else's, and my battalion opened up his wine cellar. We thought we had days to get ready. And what a wine collection! But just about dusk, we heard gunfire and motorcycles. The party was over."

"Michiel," Herbert tugged at Jan's son. "Let's go play again."

"I want to hear," Michiel answered.

"The Germans started shelling our screens before dawn. Their artillery destroyed our phone lines on the ground, and the radio in the front screens had no working batteries! So our own artillery shot from far back, with no guidance from us.

"I got shelled the next day behind the horn-work, so I can tell you how it feels." Jan wiped his brow, where little threads of sweat had formed. "It's hard to keep your head up and fire, hard not to panic and run. There's really no place to run, because the corporals are behind with pistols, ready to shoot deserters." Jan tried to smile. "Even us captains."

No one laughed, and he continued. "But still I saw a few men running. Actually running was more dangerous, out in the open, out of the trenches."

He looked out the window and moved his fingers along his hairline to daub the perspiration.

"Tell us," Roos said.

Jan sipped more coffee and raked the cup's under-rim against the saucer. "On its way in, each shell whistles, then your hole shakes from the impact. You hope each shell is the last, even though you know better.

"Anyway, I don't know what time the Germans went into our front screens. In the distance they looked like an ant army, swarming up and down the line."

Each time that Jan looked out the window, he lowered his voice.

"It took the Germans all day to clear the screens." Jan paused again and daubed his forehead. "Every defender still free and unwounded reached the horn-work by seven o'clock, I'd guess. Now the Germans were near the main line, and I heard skirmishing all night along the Grift.

"It was midnight when I reported to Colonel Hennink. General Harberts was there, too. The General couldn't believe the front screens had fallen to 'a hundred Germans.' He kept saying that: 'a hundred Germans.' From the hilltop command post where the General was, trees hid the attackers. Only men close to the front screens could see their real numbers. Harberts ordered Colonel Hennink to send the men who left the front screens up the Rhine to retake their positions, and to order our machine gunners to shoot anyone who retreated again. But Hennink, thank God, wasn't going to.

"Anyway, General Harberts was already losing control. It's not surprising — continuous action with no sleep, one cup of coffee after another, smoking cigars to keep going. Harberts was relieved of command before the surrender."

Anna looked up in alarm. "What's that noise?"

Roos spoke crossly. "What noise?"

"I'm sure I heard footsteps."

Sophia stepped to the door, and opened it to see Anneke van Oostveen. The dairyman's wife looked startled. "I'm going into Rhenen," she said as if apologizing. "Your mother-in-law's sleeping now. I just wanted to tell you. Do you need anything?"

Sophia exhaled. "No, thank you. Jan was telling us about his battle; we heard you and worried some German was listening."

"Sorry."

"It's all right." Sophia closed the door gently and stepped back to her seat.

"Would everyone be more comfortable at our house?" Anna asked.

"We're fine," Roos answered. "Go on, Jan. We're listening."

Jan looked out the window, edgy from the interruption.

"The next morning, starting before dawn, Germans shelled the horn-work for nine hours."

Maarten echoed, "Nine hours!"

"Nine hours. In the hospital later I learned the Germans used forty-eight guns; we had only a few old cannon from the 1870's." Jan laughed bitterly. "Our guns had no ballast, so they bounced back from the recoil. We built a mound behind each gun to let gravity pull it back after a shot. I think a German piece fired twenty times to each of ours."

Maarten winced.

"Just after noon, two SS battalions stormed the horn-work. By late afternoon they had it. Immediately we blew the bridge, but the charge did not destroy it."

Jan looked at his feet and paused.

"The Germans swarmed across to bypass the barbed wire and our porcupines. After they disabled the bunkers from behind, it was just a nasty infantry fight in the woods, with no defensive advantage anymore. Our rifles were all single-shot; the Germans had automatics or semiautomatics."

Anna asked, "Why did you keep fighting? Did you think you could win?"

"No one wanted to lose the battle that would cost us the war. We knew the troops behind us needed time to man the New Waterline. A lot of us thought the French and maybe the British would arrive any hour. There were all kinds of rumors. When we ran out of coffee, someone said we were saving the coffee for the French. The French were coming up the Rhine, and everyone knew the French wouldn't fight without coffee." Jan leaned forward. "But also, there's something hard in admitting defeat after such a struggle. My first day as a prisoner was the worst day of my life."

He looked around, as if wanting some acknowledgment.

"By midnight the *Moffen* cleared the hill all the way south to the Rhine. Only our last reserves kept the Germans out of Rhenen. Hennink sent me north to help the 19th Regiment scout a counterattack on our old positions. Just after dawn, we attacked with four battalions from the north. But the north reach was the one approach that was clear; we had no cover at all, while the Germans were entrenched on the hill. *Stuka* dive-bombers screaming with sirens came at us over the open ground as we charged."

Jan checked the Germans through the window.

"That's the last thing I remember; I never felt any pain. I remember seeing the *Stukas*, then waking up at nightfall in a German field hospital."

Jan took a deep breath and scanned their faces. "Have you ever been unconscious?"

All of them shook their heads no.

"When you first start to revive, you don't know where you are. For a moment, you don't know *who* you are. In fact at the very beginning you're not sure *what* you are. It's strange and unpleasant."

He looked away. Roos touched him. "What else, Jan?"

Jan licked his dry lips and sipped a little more coffee.

"Harberts was under incredible pressure. The government hadn't let him prepare, and there he was: defending our critical point with defenses half done, using outdated weapons against a lot more men." Jan shook his head. "History will make him the scapegoat. But I think I understand what he was going through."

Anna asked, "How did they treat you in the German prison?"

"Not badly. We lived in a stockade near Kiel. The food was enough: *zuurkool* and *roggebrood*, sausages, thin milk."

Roos broke in. "Thin milk? Sophia gives wounded *Moffen* cream! She nursed one in the guest bed!"

56

Sophia said, "Roos, you keep mentioning that. But could you really not save him yourself? He's twenty years old."

"Anyway, it's not fair to blame Sophia," Maarten joked. "It's probably more accurate to say *I* saved his life. Sophia only called for me."

Roos asked, "Which one is he, anyway?"

Sophia pointed through the window. "The tall one. Over there."

"By the shed? Talking to the other?"

"That's the one: Lieutenant Guse, the Colonel's adopted son. He follows me a little. And plays with Herbert."

"I'd never allow that!"

"Then send Jan over, now that he's back. Herbert needs to be around men, and he won't watch Bart milk cows." Sophia's voice had a harder edge than she had intended.

Maarten cleared his throat. "What news of Willem?"

Sophia's voice softened. "I think Willem's alive in England."

"He was in the Queen's Guard reserve," Jan agreed. "It wouldn't be surprising for his unit to evacuate with the government."

Sophia mastered the impulse to mention the "*mi tio*" broadcast.

Anna said, "Willem must be worried sick."

"I'm sure it's hard for him."

"I miss him," Maarten smiled sadly, like a comic actor stepping out of character. "We had some wild university days. All the Leiden bars knew us. And we were cycling and skating even then; it cleared the alcohol."

Everyone smiled.

Maarten looked at Sophia more cheerfully. "Remember the night in Leiden when the four of us stayed up till dawn? Willem and I bought those three-liter bottles of *Deugniet*. That night, I knew I'd marry Anna, and Willem told me the next day that he knew he'd marry you."

Maarten went on. "Did you know, Sophia, the night before your wedding, a crowd of us took Willem to the Red Light District in Amsterdam? Willem was dressed as a clown."

"Maarten, the children!" Roos interrupted.

"I think they stopped listening after the dive bombers," Sophia answered.

Maarten glanced at the children, now clustered away in the corner playing cards. "We drank beer after beer. Then we took him to the ugliest whore on the street, and paid her double."

Sophia's face must have shown her displeasure, because Maarten hurried his story.

"Willem danced with her in the window for all of us to see. I think he wanted to make sure no bad reports came back to you. Every time she drew the curtains, he pulled them back and danced some more, calling for beers which we handed him through the doorway he kept open."

Now Sophia was laughing. Jan smiled too as the memory came back.

Jan said, "Remember the time, before you had children, all six of us crowded onto Willem's silly little boat? The wooden boat he put in the shed when he went to school? We motored up the Rhine to Arnhem for dinner, and on the way back we got caught in the rain. Tiny engine, motoring four knots in hard rain. We could have *sailed* home faster!"

"Paddled!"

"Walked!"

Anna changed the subject. "Well, even without Willem, we can all be together again for Sinterklaas."

"Oh, I think we should get together still," Sophia answered. "Do you think we should all come here, as usual?"

Roos said, "Of course! Let's show the *Moffen* life in Holland goes on."

December, 1940

Women and children in oranges, reds and greens lined the Rhine wharf. Away from the dockside, men wearing their drab everydays held flasks of *jenever*. Sophia led Geertruide and Herbert to the water to see a black-bottomed wooden *stoomboot*, with an orange-and-white top-structure, moving near. At its bow stood white-bearded Sinterklaas in his cardinal's robe, a bright red miter on his head, a golden staff in his grip.

Children and mothers called, "*Dag, Sinterklaasje, dag!*"

Next to Sinterklaas, black-faced Zwarte Piet wore green velvet pantaloons, and a gold velvet jerkin with green shoulders and gold trim. A great, white ruffle circled his neck. A green and gold cap with gold and white feathers topped his head. Enormous green and gold tassels lavished his shoe-tops. Zwarte Piet shook his black wig and smiled like a lunatic with his huge, white-painted lips.

"*Dag, Zwarte Pietje, dag!*" the women and children called out.

Zwarte Piet danced clownishly while Sinterklaas stood erect, wise as any Buddha, and waved solemnly as the boat slowed. Sophia watched Herbert's face, spellbound at the sight of Sinterklaas, venerable celebrity who sailed each year from Spain to visit the children of Holland. Geertruide smiled with her bright eyes at Sinterklaas and Zwarte Piet, as if trying to guess the men behind the disguises.

Zwarte Piet threw candies in bright wrappings toward the docks. The *stoomboot* stopped, rocking from the rhythm of its own waves. Sinterklaas stepped carefully onto the wooden wharf, steadying himself on the Burgemeester's arm, then mounted a white horse, careful with his great robes.

Zwarte Piet tossed more candy in spangled parabolas, then mounted a smaller black horse in a quick leap, and the Burgemeester led Sinterklaas and Zwarte Piet into Rhenen. Children still jumped after Zwarte Piet's candy, even skeptical Geertruide bending to the ground when it fell near. Some people followed Sinterklaas and Zwarte Piet all the way to the *Gemeentehuis* but Sophia, Roos and Anna drifted away.

"I'll watch the children," Roos said. "You two have some errands, I know."

Sophia and Anna walked to Mr. Bloem's stall. His face brightened to see them.

"We're looking for Sinterklaas toys," Sophia said.

Mr. Bloem opened a wooden box of carved dwarves with skin painted yellow, varnished to the point that the wood seemed translucent. Each dwarf had a shock of multi-colored hair: flame-red with streaks of black; corn-silk with streaks of pine-green.

"These are splendid! Where are they from?"

"Austria, near the Swiss border."

Sophia handed Mr. Bloem two of the new government's guilders and turned with Anna to leave. She noticed the German lieutenant Reinhard Guse a hundred meters away, watching.

There had been no discussion. Was it just a pleasant coincidence that no Germans were near? Or had they made themselves respectfully absent?

Maarten and Jan moved between the great hall and the dining room, bluish smoke billowing from their cigars, hosting in Willem's place the gathered fathers.

Sophia stood with the women in the opening to the center hall. They scanned the children, sitting on the black and white tiles, impatient for Sinterklaas.

"The children must have exhausted themselves outside," Anna said.

"Just wait till they see Sinterklaas," Roos answered. "They'll get their energy back."

"Look at their clothes, soaking from the mist. Do you think they're warm enough?"

"It's plenty warm in here."

Roos passed a tray of *koekjes* among the mothers. Anna stood by Sophia, and asked, "Where's your mother-in-law?"

"She may come down."

"Is she getting better?"

"She recognizes me but not my name. Sometimes she smells of urine. I am paying Bart's wife to be her companion."

"Bart's wife?"

"Mrs. van Oostveen. You've seen her. She's the kindest person in Holland." Sophia turned back to the children. "Look at Geertruide."

Abandoning all skepticism, at the window Geertruide shouted, "*Sinterklaas komt!*"

A knock reverberated. Anna skipped to the massive door, opening it slowly, as if with reverence. A white-bearded Sinterklaas strode solemnly in, offering a dignified wave as he strode to his seat of honor in the high-backed oaken chair, in front of the carved fireplace of Indonesian mahogany. Zwarte Piet followed, lively as ever, but today threw no candy.

Geertruide moved close to Sophia and said, "Sinterklaas has a different face from the man at the river." Geertruide stared again. "He's the Farm Inspector, isn't he?"

"Ssh!"

Zwarte Piet handed Sinterklaas the great black book, and Sinterklaas turned the brittle page, his voice commanding as he peered into the little crowd. "Is Michiel Poel here?"

Roos' son stood and walked to the front, and Sinterklaas put a hand on his shoulder. "Now Michiel, you're very good at riding horses, aren't you."

The mothers traded smiles, as Roos pretended to answer for him. "Oh, indeed I am, Sinterklaas! How flattering that someone so prestigious knows!"

"But you don't like to clean your room, do you?" Sinterklaas's voice broke through Roos' whispering. Michiel shrank a little, and shook his head.

"Very well!" Sinterklaas cheered up. "Are you leaving your shoes out tonight? What little presents can I put in them?"

Michiel straightened up again, pleased with this question. "I want a book about planets."

"Book about planets! Oh, those are very rare, and hard to get." Sinterklaas frowned. "I'll see what I can do. Look in your shoes tomorrow! Off you go!"

Zwarte Piet leaned close to Sinter Klaas and whispered. Sinterklaas nodded and called, "Herbert van Dordrecht!"

"Look!" Roos nudged Sophia as Herbert walked to the front, his shoulders back and eyes shining. "He loves to meet celebrities!"

All of Sinterklaas' ancient wisdom came to his face as he leaned close to Herbert. "Herbert, I understand you're an extraordinary footballer; is that true?"

"His skin is barely large enough to contain him," Sophia whispered to the women.

Herbert nodded.

"But you don't always listen to your older sister, do you!" Sinterklaas spoke with kind omniscience. Herbert agreed, with no evident shame.

"Now, Herbert, what do you want on my birthday tomorrow?"

Herbert looked for a moment. "Can you bring my father home?"

Michiel snickered, and the other children started to buzz.

"What did he say?" Sophia and the women stopped smiling.

Sinterklaas' face drooped. "Want to see your father." Sinterklaas repeated the wish, buying time.

Then Sinterklaas whispered, so softly that Sophia had to strain to hear him. "Herbert, your father is in England, guarding the beloved Queen, helping her prepare to return. Now, Sinterklaas is old, and slow; I can't bring your father back this year. But I make you a promise: your father will come home. And I will tell him you asked."

PAINT ON CANVAS
February, 1941

Was it really possible that Colonel Schussler had taken such a risk? To avoid the censors, Schussler had given his letter directly to General Langer, and Langer had delivered it to Erwin unopened. If Langer had violated Schussler's trust and opened the letter, surely it would have ended Schussler's career.

Dear Erwin,

> *I write because these are feelings that I have to share, with someone. You know I am recruiting Poles to fight against the Bolsheviks. But my work is impossible now. The Gestapo and SS are organizing Einsatzgruppen to burn villages. They round up civilians and shoot them, often for nothing. I protested to my superior but he said it was out of his hands.*

> *Erwin, you know that I do not shrink at violence or avoid danger. But this is not soldiering. This is despicable. I fear for the impact on my lieutenants.*
> *Please write. Perhaps you have more cheerful news.*
>
> *Yours,*
> *Horst Schussler*

Einsatzgruppen. Erwin scowled, mouthing the word. *Ersatzgruppen* would be more accurate. Keep these imitators out and let genuine soldiers win the war. With honor.

Erwin opened his diary and made a note to himself:

Must see Langer about Poland. But do not compromise Schussler.

Carefully he placed the letter in its envelope, and buried it second to the bottom of the stack in his locker.

That night Erwin dreamed that he was back in Poland, with Schussler still his friend and rival. In his dream, the Polish day grayed into dusk, the sun bluing before it touched the horizon, its light and warmth gone while it still floated above the horizon. From the ground a rhythm began, until the rhythm became small things moving, actual creatures, animal-like and scurrying, growing larger. Then Schussler was gone and Erwin was alone, the only human. The creatures came nearer and larger until they were upright, some bent and moving in fear of the others, the others who were ghoulish figures dancing to the rhythm which had formed them all, terrifying the bent forms fleeing them. Erwin could not control the movement of his legs and stood frozen like a tree, moaning.

Poland was not as he had left it: a place instead of coldness, of evil spirits unconquerable, unknowable, inescapable.

Erwin awoke. He remembered he had dreamt of Poland, of unspeakable evil, but could not conjure the images, could not verbalize the dream.

He rushed outside into the familiar Holland air, cool and damp and full of life. He looked with relief at the linden trees tilting in the wind.

Anna and Sophia walked with Herbert and Geertruide in the February air. In the bleak distance, leafless trees looked like brown snowflakes. The mist seemed to have blanched the green and orange and red from the distant buildings, melding all into a universal drear.

Sophia said, "Children, can you feel the wind? Feel how strong it is?"

"Yes," Herbert answered. "It's strong."

"Do you know what the wind is?"

"What, mamma?"

"God's whispering. The wind is God's whisper, to show he is near you."

Geertruide and Herbert gusted away in a sprint.

Anna smiled at Sophia. "I never knew you were so devout."

Sophia breathed out a little chuckle. "Who knows what to say to children? I can't tell them what's happened here, in words they'll understand. I'm afraid they'll see the world as uncontrollable, unknowable. If it has to be beyond their understanding, how awful if they think it's malevolent. I don't know how they'd ever recover from that."

After the walk they made tea, and carried the hot cups into the greenhouse.

"I'm sure you've heard," Anna said. "Seyss-Inquart ordered all Jews to register on January 10. In the larger towns, they're deporting them. Amsterdam workers went on strike to protest."

"I heard something, but nothing recent."

"The strike is petering out. The Nazis are arresting leaders. Amsterdammers will strike for the Jews, but they won't die for them."

"Weren't there also anti-Jewish riots?"

"Mostly Nazis."

"German Nazis, or local NSB?"

"Both, I'm sure. But there are so many more NSB. Their leader Mussert must feel he has a lot to prove."

Sophia shook her head.

"You know the NSB bureau in town?"

"On *Hoogestraat*, next to the *Gemeentehuis*."

They sat, quiet for a moment.

Anna's eyes wandered from the greenhouse door to a painted canvas, with a near-finished trio of apples: rose and green and yellow against the dark wooden platter.

"Sophia, your painting is incredible. It looks more like real apples than a photograph would. The coloring . . . it's not really true to the model. The color on the canvas makes it better, more real."

"Thank you."

"Maarten says a drop of water in whiskey unlocks the flavor. I put a pinch of dill on salmon, and there's more salmon flavor than if I served it plain. It's the same way with your colors."

Sophia's face made its expressive flower, and she laughed. "Thank you for saying that. It's exactly what I try to do."

"But Sophia, how can you concentrate enough to paint, in a time like this?"

"Anna, how can I not? If I stop creating, who knows what might happen to me? Painting saves me from becoming driftwood."

Anna gave the look that made Sophia love her so much, the look of amused admiration that made Sophia feel someone saw into her mind and understood her.

Anna rose. "Oh, well. Maarten will be home from the clinic by now."

Sophia stayed alone in the greenhouse, using candles to enhance the dwindling light, painting. She studied a mint plant in a little flowerpot. The plant was already outlined on her canvas. Now she embellished and varied the greens on the palette. The outline on the canvas perfectly copied the living plant; with form she was precise. But, just as Anna had said, with color Sophia indulged herself, used a slow patience to mix and test the shades. She mixed and remixed, and dabbed to the canvas, until the plant on the canvas looked more like the living one than a more faithful copy might.

Erwin looked up from the forms on his desk, and stared through the library's rear window, through the mist, and through the greenhouse window, over Sophia's shoulder. Away from her, he put her out of his mind. But meeting her now always flustered him a little. He tried to seem nonchalant, and found himself acting very correct. After she left, he found himself rehearsing the things he should have said.

April, 1941

The Sunday sky hung low and misty. Old people walked or bicycled in church clothes, draped in wool coats for the lingering cold, oblivious to the mist.   On Paardenveld's front lawn Sophia bent and picked up scattered leaves, filling a basket on her elbow.

On the river road the Germans Strohn and Vogel approached. Between them, in hand-cuffs, a young Netherlander tried to look unafraid, though his eyes were pinched and forlorn. He returned Sophia's gaze momentarily, then looked away.

Erwin met them outside. He spoke to the Netherlander, too low for Sophia to hear. The Netherlander shook his head, and Erwin gestured to the woods. Strohn and Vogel led the young man across the bridge behind the house, and into the trees.

Erwin walked toward Sophia. Just as he neared, she heard a gunshot from the woods. The gunshot's clear report shocked her and she fell to her knees.

Erwin grasped her hand. "We found him carrying explosives. Military law is clear: a spy in civilian clothes is shot or hanged. I said we would spare his life if he named other resisters for us. He refused."

Erwin tugged at her arm to help her rise. "He died instantly, with no pain. My instructions are to send men like him to Germany for full interrogation. You can be sure this was kinder."

He lingered, as if waiting for her to speak. When she didn't, he turned and entered the house.

July 1941

The bright July sun gleamed through the library windows, lapping General Langer and Erwin with its rays. Erwin asked, "How goes the Russian invasion?"

"We're killing and capturing whole divisions," Langer answered happily. "Our only limit is fuel and supply."

"Did the timing surprise you?"

"No. We had to attack this year, before Stalin could rearm. And it had to be after the spring thaw, but early enough to win before the freeze."

Langer looked out the window. "It would have been better to start even sooner, but this Italian fiasco in Greece . . . there was no choice but for us to move resources south. I wish we had started weeks ago."

Erwin cleared his throat. "I might have waited. I would have gotten England out of the war first, one way or the other."

"Most of the generals agree with you. But so far, the result has vindicated Hitler each time. Remember the Rhineland. Then Austria. Then Czechoslovakia. Hitler moved, and the World stood by. Everyone thought Poland would bring an earthquake, but England and France never fired a shot. Who but Hitler would have ventured into Norway? Hitler moved and it fell. France! France . . ." Langer shook his head. "The fastest victory over a World Power in human history. Hitler has an intuition . . ."

After a silence, Langer changed the subject. "When does your group assemble?"

Erwin checked his watch. "Twenty minutes. I planned a short speech. Then I'll leave them alone for their farewell dinner."

Erwin paced on the front lawn with General Langer, reviewing the first Hollandish graduates. He walked the five lines of twenty, eyeing them from head to toe, measuring them, looking for any lapse. He found none. The Netherlanders were ready. He found himself glancing at Langer to see if his mentor felt the same satisfaction.

Back in front, Erwin began to speak to this historical group, his voice just loud enough to be sure they heard.

"Monday you leave to fight the Bolsheviks, with your first leaders, Vogel and Strohn. In Russia you will join the largest battle in the history of the Earth. You have either prepared by now or you have not; I have nothing left to teach you.

"Except one thing.

"Remember always to use the extremest violence. War is violent by nature. This seems clear and obvious, but many soldiers forget. In its extremest form, violence destroys the brave enemy, and terrorizes the timid one. The great soldiers have always understood this. When you come near the Russians, make yourself an agent of the extremest violence."

His eyes scanned their faces. "At stake is the future of the World. You can lay the foundation for the greatest civilization in history. A rare adventure awaits you; a great victory is yours to claim."

He stepped away to signal the end of his speech, gesturing to Vogel and Strohn. The three stepped away and he spoke softly to them.

"When you go east, find Colonel Schussler if you can. Schussler commanded one of the Panzer regiments that entered Estonia. His assignment recently changed. He is an old friend of mine, and if he knows who you are, he will try to meet you and look after you."

Strohn and Vogel nodded.

"One more thing." Erwin hesitated. "There is a rumor that special units in the East are killing women and children. Not just reprisals, but wholesale. I think it is misinformation. But if you find this kind of killing after you arrive, send me a letter. To get past the censors, just write, 'It is true.' I'll know your meaning."

They sat outside, the five remaining Myrmidons with five new brothers-in-arms, the best of the Netherlanders now made lieutenants, all at the great oak table in the garden, relishing the July air, handling big, tubular beer glasses. Nagel, though senior to them all, happily played cook and waiter. He raked three empty beer glasses across the table together, and asked, "*Ein maß?*"

"*Ja, bitte,*" Strohn answered him. "*Vom Fass!*" The others laughed, remembering the print advertisement of Germany's first nationally advertised beer. *Vom Fass!* From the keg! As if that were somehow special. It sounded childlike, even in the advertisements, and Strohn's tone mocked it perfectly.

Nagel brought a tray of filled glasses, and the men laughed louder as the foam settled. The levity, and the volume of their talk, spiraled upward as the beer went down.

Then Nagel brought a great platter of sausages, with dishes of mustard and sauerkraut. "My mother sent these," Kessler said.

Glowing, Zimmer explained to the new comrades, "*Nurnberger* bratwursts, very special, preserved in brine. Captain Nagel has boiled them in beer and then broiled them. Very special."

Through the window from inside, Erwin and Langer watched them all.

"The vision is becoming real," Langer said.

"These new officers are as good as the Myrmidons were at the same stage," Erwin answered.

It was more than that. They showed the same delight in their skills, the same purpose and fulfillment, the same sense of being connected to something larger than themselves. It made conversation with them easy and pleasurable; they were brothers of the highest order. Erwin saw it all, the respect they showed the Myrmidons, and the deference the Myrmidons showed them in return. All of them, he thought, had lost the illusion of individuality that prevents human understanding, and had bonded in purpose and spirit.

Erwin could not resist stepping outside, and Langer followed.

"Gentlemen," Erwin began. "A toast to the first expedition of Netherlanders. In a few short months, I will be reading letters from Russia about the heroism of these men."

He smiled, but it was clear that his toast was not a joke. It was a prediction.

Warm with pride and beer, the men at the table raised their near-empty glasses in response.

September, 1941

Erwin drove with Kessler, Zimmer and Guse to Lichtenvoorde to see for himself what was wrong. At the recruiting booth, local men came alone or in small groups, browsed the posters and pamphlets, said nothing, and left.

Guse showed photographs of the hundred Netherlanders who had left for Russia that summer.

"This one came from Lichtenvoorde," Guse said, pointing. Some nodded, but gave the photographs only vacant looks. They said nothing, and left.

"It's different now," Zimmer said.

"The mistrust is worse than 1940."

Kessler opened a notebook. "Six weeks, moving the booths from *dorp* to *dorp*, five volunteers. Last year we took only the best hundred and turned away the rest. We didn't even take their names, we were so sure they would reapply. Now where are they?"

"Five men in six weeks," Guse scowled. "Probably just men without work."

Erwin frowned. "If this is the limit, I need to tell General Langer. I doubt this work can justify our absence from the battlefield."

Erwin's first speech to the new class went badly. He spoke the same words as the year before, but he could not rekindle last year's passion for such an ordinary little group. His words did not even stir any emotions inside himself, and it was clear he was boring them. They nodded politely, as if trying to help him along in his struggling little speech. He skipped parts, and hurried to the end.

Despite the speech's embarrassing failure, he tried a new tactic, and came directly among them. When they lurched to attention, he laughed and said, "Not yet. You can relax. Drill and posture come later. Tell me your names."

As they answered, he found his mind wandering again, until they finished. Then he said, "Last summer, so many more men applied. Why?"

The men shook their heads, blankly. Erwin tried to hide his impatience. These lumps probably didn't know. Otherwise, maybe they were afraid to say anything that seemed critical of the Germans. Finally, a balding man, almost too heavy to be accepted, leaned forward and spoke with an insulting familiarity. "There is much propaganda in circulation, from the underground presses."

Erwin tried to hide his dislike of the man. "What are they saying?"

"Oh, you can imagine. Playing up the Jewish regulations, the Amsterdam strikers. Always exaggerated. They circulate a stolen letter written by a German officer in Poland, complaining about mass executions there."

Erwin felt his face go flush. Was his redness visible to the others? He answered too quickly. "A letter? From a German in Poland? Addressed to whom?"

"The salutation's crossed out. But it's signed. I was sure it was fake. But many people talk about it."

Beads of sweat formed under Erwin's hat band. He removed the hat and swabbed his temple. "It's unusually hot."

Had Schussler's letter fallen into enemy hands? How many copies must they have made? He wanted to rush inside, to check his locker.

In the sewing room, Geertruide helped Herbert build a castle with blocks. Sophia replayed in her mind last Sunday's Radio *Oranje* broadcast.

Erwin Schell appeared in the doorway. "You took a letter from my office."

Sophia did not rise. "What?"

"I had a letter from an officer in Poland. It's missing. You're the only one who could have taken it."

"You shoot people who do things like that. Do you imagine I would take such a ridiculous risk, with two children to raise?"

"No one else could have!" Erwin stared at her, as if actually seeing her for the first time. "You invaded my private belongings and stole from me."

Sophia laughed bitterly. "Sir! I invaded your property, and stole from you! Think of what you are saying!"

Geertruide's face was fixed upward, watching them. Herbert had already returned to his blocks.

November, 1941

On the first clear day since September, the sunlight streamed through the library glass windows. Guse stood by the chair opposite Erwin's desk. Sitting would have broken protocol, except in a full meeting with other officers.

"This isn't business," Erwin told him. "You're my son. Sit. *Bitte.*"

Guse took the chair.

"You're starting your second autumn here."

"Yes," Guse smiled. "I wonder if I'm slowly becoming a Netherlander."

Erwin pulled a letter from a stack of envelopes. "I thought you'd enjoy this letter. It's from Strohn in Russia."

Guse unfolded and read aloud.

Dear Colonel Schell

As you may know, Vogel and I serve under Manstein, near the Don. Four of our Netherlanders already wear medals. All who serve with them speak of their courage and skill.

We did not have to look for Colonel Schussler as you suggested; he instead found us. He said it's not surprising that Netherlanders trained by you should fight well; he called you his only real rival. His own Polish recruits are also well regarded.

Our best wishes to Guse, to Zimmer, and to Kessler.

Sincerely,
Dichter Strohn

"That's wonderful." Guse handed the letter back to Erwin. "The experiment's succeeding. It's too bad the recruiting here goes so slowly."

Erwin folded the letter and replaced it in the stack. "We may defeat Russia before winter. Or the U-boats may force England to surrender. Then our eventual victory will be obvious again, as it was in 1940, and the recruiting will accelerate."

Erwin pulled another letter from the stack. "From Colonel Schussler himself."

Guse read aloud.

Dear Erwin

I congratulate you on your program's success. I met the Germans you sent east: Strohn and Vogel. They are men of the first rank. I must tell you that when they first arrived, they made a strange impression by their insistence on carrying swords . . .

Here Guse and Erwin exchanged knowing smiles.

. . . Now everyone speaks well of them. They are always at the front line whenever the enemy is present. They will not be wasted in the service of Manstein, who succeeds everywhere against the Russians.

I've also heard how well your Netherlanders perform. Some of their names have appeared in communications to Berlin!

We miss your presence, and I hope to see Reinhard Guse soon.

Yours,
Horst Schussler

Erwin looked intently at his adopted son. "It's all a tribute to you, Reinhard. You and the other lieutenants. This program is mine in name, but you men executed the training. You should be extremely proud."

"Thank you."

"Oh, well." Erwin leaned back now. "How will you spend your Sunday?"

Guse smiled self-consciously. "I play ball with the boy Herbert, as you know. We walk into town and kick the ball in the little park. Other children gradually join us. Sometimes it turns into a full-day affair. I always join the weaker team and play at half speed. They think it's wonderful to play with someone my age."

Guse laughed. "Just to get them excited, I told them I once played on the German national team. I meant it as a kind of joke, but they believed it. They talk as if I'm a celebrity."

"Your time with those boys helps create goodwill for us."

"Probably."

They sat across the desk from each other in a comfortable silence, and then Guse stood to go.

Erwin scanned Guse's maturing frame. "Have a good game, then."

Guse made a respectful nod and stepped out.

Erwin pulled a third letter from the stack and read it again.

Dear Colonel Schell,

It's true.

   Sincerely,
   Uwe Vogel

January, 1942

Monsieur Marc Lenoir
77 Rue St. Simon

Arrondissement VI
Paris, France

Dear Marc,

  Sorry I haven't written more. You can't imagine the situation here. We still assume Willem's in England but no word. His mother still doesn't know us. I worry about Geertruide and Herbert in this strange environment.
  The children hardly remember you and it's a shame. It would mean a great deal to me if you could visit.

  Your loving sister,
  Sophia

The doorbell rang. Sophia folded the letter and slid it into an envelope, then trotted downstairs. Maarten stood in the doorway with Anna, grinned his conspirator's grin and handed Sophia a brown paper sack with wet sides. "We're inviting ourselves for dinner."

Sophia looked in the sack. "Rabbits?"

Maarten grinned. "Very fresh. I caught them south of the river. I have a couple of traps. Hadn't used them since I was a child."

Anna followed Sophia into the kitchen, ignoring Maarten's call for drinks. Sophia pulled out two rabbits, unwrapped the wax paper and studied the skinned, gutted and headless bodies. She cut the meat away from the bones and broke the legs into pieces, then put them into a stewpot with canned tomatoes and preserved olives.

"Your pantry must be running down," Anna said. "Soon you'll be asking your Colonel for food."

"First we'll have Anneke Van Ostveen's vegetables. Have I ever taken you to see her when she's canning?"

"No."

"Remind me to take you. It's quite an enterprise. She could feed an army with what she preserves. Mostly cabbage from Friesland."

Anna and Sophia joined Maarten in the sewing room, where he was teasing Geertruide and Herbert.

"Scoot over," Anna said to Maarten on the little sofa. Anna looked at Sophia. "It's come to Rhenen, Sophia. Jews have to wear a yellow Star of David."

"Besides Mr. Bloem, are there any Jews still in Rhenen?"

"If there are, I don't see them. You wonder why the Germans bother."

"Has Mr. Bloem put on a star?"

"He puts it on his overcoat, then forgets to bring his overcoat to the stall. You never see one on him."

"Something will happen if he's not careful."

They watched the children silently until Sophia asked, "And what are the laws on selling, now?" She was curious about Anna's little furniture store: little antiques and home decorations.

"I can't sell to anyone wearing a star."

"This order comes from Seyss-Inquart?"

Maarten answered, "I think so. Enforced locally by the NSB."

Anna added, "Of course, less than fifty guilders worth of sales ever came in a year from Jews, so we won't suffer especially. But what do you say to someone who asks to buy?"

Maarten looked at Anna. "Do you really think any Jew will suffer because he can't buy home decorations? I think they have more important worries."

"No, but they'll suffer if they can't find groceries or clothes. And if stores like mine obey the law, then grocers and tailors are isolated and they'll have to comply."

Maarten said, "It sounds cruel to ask, but what do you think the Jews would do if the roles were reversed?"

Anna answered, "They are reversed. I think it's illegal now for us to buy from their shops."

"I meant, if we were in the minority, and such an order meant we might not get the things we need?"

Sophia said, "You speak as if all Jews would answer the same way."

"But you take my point."

"It's hard to answer," Anna intervened.

"It's probably a meaningless question," Maarten said, looking at them both. "I doubt any Jew would come into the store and ask to buy something, as long as Seyss-Inquart's order is in force."

Sophia's mind wandered to last Sunday's Radio Oranje broadcast: "*El tio te ama. El tio ama sus enfantes.*" The message was too odd not to be Willem's.

"What is it, Sophia? You look distracted. We haven't upset you, I hope."

"No," she answered, looking up at them both again.

October, 1942

Monsieur Marc Lenoir
77 Rue St. Simon
Arrondissement VI
Paris, France

Dear Marc,

The last time you wrote, you said I had "disowned" our family. I assumed that you meant marrying a jonkheer and moving to the country. Was it something more serious? Is that why you don't answer my mail?

I need very much to hear from you. If this letter goes unanswered, I'll worry something terrible has happened.

Your worried sister,
Sophia

Sophia put extra stamps on the envelope to minimize the chance of a return.

"Let's go see Mrs. Van Oostveen," Sophia told the children. "I have a letter she can mail when she goes to town. The harvests are nearly finished and you can see her canning."

As they walked, Geertruide asked, "It's the big jars you showed us last year, right, mamma?"

"Yes, the great ceramic jars, taller than you. The same as you see in our pantry. She boils the jars to get all the air out, then she seals them. As the jars cool, a vacuum makes the seal airtight."

"*Zuurkool?*"

"You'll see mounds of green and red cabbage from Friesland. She'll make *zuurkool* of the green and *rodekool* of the red. But you'll see her canning other things: *snidebonen*, apples and spinach."

Sophia slowed to let the children catch up. "She even pickles eggs in brine. Anyway, you'll see it all. She wanted to show you."

They stopped before they reached the brick cottage. Bart sat on a stone with his face in his hands. Sophia had never seen Bart this way.

"Geertruide, walk Herbert back to the house. I want to see Mr. van Oostveen alone."

Herbert looked up with his dramatic eyes. "But we're going to see the canning."

Geertruide looked at Sophia as if it were not in her power to lead Herbert anywhere, but Sophia leaned close and said, "Go."

Geertruide pulled Herbert unwillingly back. Herbert's squeals of protest aroused Bart.

"*Goede morgen,*" Sophia began.

"*Morge.*" Bart's voice was flat.

"*Hoe gaat het?*" Sophia's tone demanded an answer.

Bart pulled a document from his shirt pocket, unfolded it and handed it to her. She read a conscription notice, written in the clumsy bureaucratic of Seyss-Inquart's administration: Dutch writers trying to express the ideas of German supervisors. The Fatherland needed Bart to fortify the coast against Holland's enemies.

The print wavered in Sophia's vision. Until now the prospect of liberation had always seemed too distant to imagine; the conscription notice made the image real again.

Bart breathed from deep in his stomach. "There's no time limit on this. I'm afraid I'll be away a long time."

She refolded the letter. "Maybe Colonel Schell can help."

Erwin rose as Sophia entered.

"Please." She handed him the paper. "Can you do something about this?"

His eyes crinkled as he scanned the typed form. "This is from the Reichsgovernor, a different line of authority from mine. There's nothing I can do."

He handed back the sheet. "It's temporary. Why so much concern?"

"What about his wife?"

"If you knew how unprepared the Atlantic Wall . . ." He seemed to catch himself.

"Why not rely on volunteers?"

"None would join."

"Doesn't that prove something? These 'enemies of Holland:' no actual Hollanders seem afraid of them."

Sophia rejoined Bart behind the little canal. "I'm sorry, Bart; I was wrong." She handed him the paper and took a deep breath. "Bart, take care of yourself. You know the Germans will lose, and we'll be free again. It's certain."

"What makes you certain?"

"The whole world is against them. Americans and British are in Italy. Have you tried to count the planes flying east to bomb them? We can't even conceive the resources now joined against Germany."

They looked at each other.

"So be careful, Bart. It's not for you to take risks. They would have little value, and the war will be won without them."

Bart made the slightest of nods. Sophia continued. "You don't have to worry about Anneke. I'll make sure she's provided for."

"How?"

"I buried little tin cans of money all over the property."

Bart let go a bitter laugh. Sophia held him by the elbows and spoke forcefully. "Don't worry, Bart. I'll make sure she doesn't go without."

In the window's scant afternoon light, Sophia and Anna knitted by the children.

"I wonder where it will stop," Anna said. "Only a day after I told him about Bart's conscription, Maarten showed me a summons addressed to him. But his crew is working inside Germany; he took his bicycle to Arnhem to catch a train."

"Do you have an address?"

"He said he'd write as soon as he knew."

Something outside distracted Sophia. Looking out, she saw Zimmer and Kessler escorting a young man in hand-cuffs. He must have been caught some distance away and marched to Paardenveld without a chance to change, because against the deepening cold he wore only a wool jacket and a dark, olive-green cap with a gold-colored shield patch. He wore the same forlorn look as the first spy the Germans had caught . . . had it been a year ago already?

Sophia tried to cue Anna but could not, without alerting the children. So she watched the prisoner from the corner of her eye.

"Has Jan gotten a summons?" she asked as she watched.

"Not the last time I saw Roos, just last Saturday. With Jan's military record, you'd think he'd be the first to get picked up."

This prisoner: had Sophia seen him with Bart? Yes, probably. In fact, before the war Bart had told her that the man said Sophia looked Jewish.

The captive seemed unaware of her watching, as Zimmer and Kessler led him to the door. What had they found him carrying? Would this one choose a bullet to the forehead, or agree to betray Holland? What a choice!

After they were through the door, Sophia listened for any voices from the office, but heard nothing. Herbert wanted attention; she stroked him gently without taking particular note of his presence. She drew the curtains closer and watched outside through the narrowed opening.

"It is strange," she said to Anna, "that they took Maarten and Bart, but left Jan free."

"Let's hope Jan's not next."

"I haven't seen Roos in weeks," Sophia said. It had been months, actually.

"She frets about the war," Anna said. "You know Roos. She lives completely in the present. Very hard for her to imagine a future with the Germans gone, and wait."

"You see her often?"

"We shop."

"She never invites me these days," Sophia said.

Anna hesitated. "What is it?" Sophia asked.

Anna looked down, then up again into Sophia's eyes. "It bothers her how you tolerate the Germans, Sophia."

"Tolerate them? What does she expect me to do? Abandon my husband's house to them?"

"I think it's more than that. She thinks you're friendly with them."

"How does she know I'm not spying on them and sending all kinds of secrets straight to England?"

Anna smiled. "Don't lose your temper. I almost didn't tell you because I thought it would create friction between you two."

Sophia still gazed through the gap in the curtains. Zimmer and Kessler walked the young Hollander back outside, now without hand-cuffs. The man lingered a moment to talk; the faces of the three men were earnest, but not hostile. Then the Netherlander left in the direction he had come, tightening his inadequate coat and pulling his olive-green cap low on his forehead.

This one had saved his life somehow. What had he promised the Germans?

November, 1942

Herbert's face was red from the cold, and water ran from his eyes. As she looked closely, Sophia saw these were not wind-tears but crying ones.

"Herbert, what's wrong?"

"I wanted Michiel to join us, but Tantje Roos won't let him."

"Why not?"

"Because Lieutenant Guse plays."

"Let's go see."

Sophia bundled for the cold and walked with Herbert to the field at the edge of town. For ten minutes she watched the boys swarm around Guse, then walked alone up cobble-stoned Regulierstraat, to the Poels' door.

When she'd first come to Rhenen years before, Sophia had not immediately liked Roos. Roos then had seemed so ... local: speaking with the self-assurance of the untraveled, throwing out opinions on topics she knew little about.

Then a rumor had surfaced that Sophia was Jewish, that Willem had brought her away to Rhenen to hide her past. A vague aloofness settled like a veil around the shopkeepers and church congregation.

Roos' response had been emphatic: her best friend, Sophia Vaubin van Dordrecht, was certainly not Jewish, and even if she were, it was nobody's business. The next market day Roos shopped publicly with Sophia until closing; that Sunday, Jan and Roos sat next to Sophia in church. Though lacking the double surname of old *jonkheer* families, Poels had lived in Rhenen since the thirteenth century, and locally no name was more prestigious. The warmth of the shopkeepers and congregation had returned.

Now the curtains at the Poel house were drawn. Sophia clapped the brass knocker loudly against its base three times before Roos opened the door.

"*Dag.*" Sophia's tone was more challenging than she had intended.

"*Goede morgen.*" Sophia had heard Roos use this correct tone before, to a shopkeeper she would never buy from again.

"Herbert says you won't let Michiel play in the park."

It was the first time ever that Roos did not invite her in from the cold, but only spoke through the half-opened door. "These friends of yours are Holland's enemies!"

"Let the Army get them out."

"It's your country, too. Not just the Army's."

"No one else is protecting my children. If that means letting Germans be kind to my son, then I will."

Roos' eyes seemed to release Sophia from any connection. "You are a coward and a traitor."

Sophia tried to control her anger. "Roos, take a deep breath."

A strange hostility glinted from Roos' eyes. Unable to stand it, Sophia said, "If you insist on speaking that way, it will be impossible for us to be friends."

"If you see nothing wrong in playing with *Moffen*, then it already is impossible."

Neither of them knowing what to say, Roos began to close the door. For the shortest instant, their faces relaxed and showed something of their old affection. Then their mouths tightened again into correctness and pain. The door closed solidly against the wooden frame, and the iron bolt clicked.

THE MIDDLE OF THE WAR
April, 1943

Sophia looked up from brewing tea and saw Bart's wife standing in the kitchen doorway. For the first time Sophia could remember, Anneke van Oostveen's tired eyes were bright.

"Come see your mother-in-law."

"What is it?"

The *boerin*'s toothy smile broadened. "Come see."

Sophia followed her upstairs to the bedroom, and found Willem's mother sitting up, braced by pillows, her white hair straight from brushing, her patterned nightgown fluffed, her face with the serenity of someone waking from a long sleep.

"Sophia," she said, too calm even to smile.

"Good afternoon," Sophia answered.

"Anneke told me everything."

"What do you remember?"

"Lots of things, but they're hazy, as if I've been in a long dream."

"I'm glad you're feeling better; we've missed you." She warned herself not to expect too much.

"What's happened?"

"Jan's home, but still no word of Willem. Bart was drafted for labor; maybe Anneke told you. England held out; the Germans quit trying and invaded Russia instead. Was that two summers ago? But they couldn't take Moscow before the freeze, and it seems a kind of stalemate now. Oh! Japan bombed Hawaii and now America's in, against Germany too."

"America." There was a silence, as if the very idea of America were new again. "That's encouraging."

"I suppose. You lose track, sometimes."

"How's Anna?"

"Fine, though Maarten was drafted for labor also."

"And Roosmarijn?"

Sophia hesitated. "Fine, I think. We don't speak." She bit her lip.

The old eyes searched Sophia's face. "What's wrong?"

"Roos thinks I'm a collaborator."

"You're joking! Why?"

"Because I nursed Lieutenant Guse's wound, and let him play *voetbal* with Herbert."

"How long?"

"It's been months."

"Sophia, that's horrible!"

Sophia felt tears in her eyes. "She wasn't my easiest friend, but my loyalest."

"If I'd been well, I'd have set this right in five minutes."

"What would you say?"

"I'd tell her she's stubborn and judgmental, sees life too simply. Just like me at her age. She'd listen to me. We're exactly the same, you know."

Sophia almost stopped herself, but the words escaped. "She's like a daughter to you," she said softly.

Her mother-in-law gripped Sophia with surprising strength. "Don't ever say that. You're the daughter; you just took some getting used to. Oh, Sophia, you're three times the woman Roos is." The old face twisted with emotion, snarling with love. "I can't imagine what I'd change about you."

She patted Sophia's shoulders. "Cheer up," she said without smiling. "I'll visit Roos tomorrow."

The massive front door slammed; Sophia imagined it was Erwin. But it was her mother-in-law instead who strode through the great hall, with a purpose she must have shown thirty years before. Sophia had to stop her to speak. "Did you see Roos?"

"Roos wasn't home. Sophia, have you seen the signs? Where Jews can shop, where they can eat, where they can sit! It's outrageous!"

"Did you also see they have to wear a star?"

"Unbelievable!"

"I wonder why they waste their time. There can't be more than a handful of Jews in the whole area."

The old woman's eyes twitched. "Do you have some yellow cloth?"

"I'm sure; why?"

"If they make any Hollander wear a star, then I'm wearing one too. They can't divide us this way." She pulled her white hair from her face and smiled defiantly. "You know, I'm still more Roosmarijn than I imagined."

Sophia slept the most contented sleep she could remember. Only now did she know how alone she had felt, with Willem gone, her father-in-law dead, the Poels not speaking to her, Maarten and Bart drafted for labor: how soon before she lost them all? The return of her mother-in-law changed everything.

Sophia carried a breakfast tray happily to her mother-in-law's room.

"I can't tell you how glad I am to have you back!"

On the bed stand lay a yellow Star of David and six loose pins. But in the bed a startled old woman cringed, then stared. Old Mevrouw Van Dordrecht's mind was gone again; the star of protest useless.

Rhenen's Jews would have to bear their indignities alone. And Roos' forgiveness would have to wait.

"Sophia, you're not yourself lately."

Was it that obvious? "Anna, was there a time when you felt you had arrived as a full-grown, capable adult who knew how to react to almost anything?"

Anna laughed. "You know, I sort of muddle through. Frankly, that's more my image of you."

Sophia almost wept. "That was my image of myself, but now that feeling seems far away, so far away that it's hard to remember ever having it."

"Sophia, think of the pressures you're under. Who on earth is 'capable' of this?"

"You remember my brother Marc?"

"From the wedding."

"He doesn't write."

"You've written him?"

"Over and over."

"Maybe the mail just doesn't get through."

"He said something to me, last time he wrote . . . said I had disowned our past. What on earth do you think that meant?"

"That is an odd thing to say. Marrying a *jonkheer*? Were the Lenoirs Huguenots?"

"We never talked about religion. I got mine in school."

Sophia forgot Anna for a moment and thought of her brother, the unsatisfied one who questioned everything. Who'd never accepted the three essential clarities: first, that life is short and therefore precious; second, that every human is independent; and, third, that to be unhappy was a kind of abdication.

Marc instead consumed by his quest to discover his "belonging," as if there were some destiny beyond the simple interaction of his past and his present, infecting every family event with his pale discontent. Marrying Willem had been a kind of escape from Marc's tragic world.

Marc's tragic world. To Paris, in search of "truth." Revealing some new insight in each letter until the last one, just after their father's funeral in Rotterdam. Sophia had disowned her heritage, Marc's letter had said.

May 15, 1943
Monsieur Marc Lenoir
77 Rue St. Simon
Arrondissement VI
Paris, France

Dear Marc,

It's been eight weeks since my letter and I'm frantic I haven't heard from you. Surely you would have sent me a note if you'd moved. If you don't reply to this one I'll probably drive to Paris, although I haven't got the slightest idea what kind of permit I might need.
I can't tell you how much it would mean to hear from you. Please write.

Love, Sophia

July, 1943

The day her mother-in-law died, Sophia was surprised to feel relief. At last the ax had cut cleanly, ending the long, gangrenous doubt. Her funeral was only a trace of the ceremony given her husband, the old doctor. Hardly any locals had seen her since she went addled, and almost no one traveled now from the North Sea coastal cities. Even the cluster of Colonel Schell's men at the grave was smaller. At the graveside Sophia felt profoundly alone.

Erwin switched off the shameless BBC, still blaring the Star-Spangled Banner after America's Independence Day. He chuckled to himself: Fourth of July, when Britain and America had split forever apart. Now desperate for a friend, the contemptible British played America's music anyway.

The telephone rang and he lifted the receiver. "*Sie sprechen mit Colonel Schell.*"

General Langer's voice sounded crisp and clear. "Erwin."

"Yes, General." It was odd; General Langer never called on the telephone.

"The greatest tank battle in history began at 4:30 this morning, north and south of the Kursk salient. We estimate four thousand Russian tanks, against three thousand of ours. The winner of this battle will win the war."

"If that's true, shouldn't I be there?"

The General paused. "I'll call you after the result is clear."

Nine days passed with no Kursk news. Berlin radio reported the Sicily landings: the first British soldiers on the Continent since Greece fell; the first Americans in the war. But from Russia still nothing.

Nagel's voice brought Erwin back to the here and now. "You look morose, Colonel; you've looked that way for weeks."

Erwin looked up. "I'm not aware of it," he said. "I'm sure I only seem that way when I'm trying to concentrate."

"Must be. Sorry to disturb you."

Erwin exhaled. It really was unacceptable for Nagel to comment on Erwin's mood. He uncapped his fountain pen and scribbled a note to admonish him, when the right time came.

On the tenth day Erwin telephoned General Langer's headquarters. At the sound of the adjutant's hello, Erwin spoke hopefully. "*Guten Tag, Kaptain Sinder. Sie sprechen mit Kolonel*

Schell." Erwin caught himself sounding more earnest than he had intended.

"*Guten Tag, Kolonel Schell.*"

"Is the General available?"

"He's in a meeting. May I ask him to call you back?"

"Of course."

But the whole day passed with no call from General Langer. All the next morning, Erwin sat again in his office, waiting. When the telephone finally rang, he buried his irritation.

"Erwin."

"General. Thank you for calling."

"Yes, of course. I was in meetings that I could not leave. I'm terribly sorry you had to wait."

"I was wondering if you had any news of Kursk."

There was a pause. "The battle was not a success."

"I'm sorry."

"Erwin, when I called you before the battle, I may have overstated its importance."

"I understand." There was another silence. Finally, Erwin said, "*Auf Wiedersehen.*"

"*Auf Wiedersehen.*"

Erwin placed the receiver on the brass hook. How soon would casualty lists be published? If Strohn or Vogel had died, Schussler would probably learn first. And Schussler would notify him, surely.

November, 1943

The weeks dragged more slowly than any Erwin could remember. Sometimes he joined the others, still combing the small towns fruitlessly for recruits. Sometimes he worked on the training manuals General Langer forwarded to Berlin. One bleak Friday at his desk, he heard a knock against his open door. Seeing Sophia, he rose reflexively. "Come in. *Bitte*."

"Where are the others?" she asked.

"Weekend passes to Amsterdam."

"The children asked me to invite you to dinner."

"The children?"

"Please come. It's too odd, a man living here and them not knowing him."

Erwin looked at her a moment. "I'd be delighted."

"Seven o'clock?"

Shaving for the second time that day, Erwin stopped imagining Vogel and Strohn in Russia and thought only of the immediate. He checked his brass buttons, then turned left and right in the mirror, looking for any ruffle. He gave his sleeve a final tug and stepped into the hallway.

In the great hall he paused at the photograph of the young doctor, this woman's lost husband, and studied the man's expression of confidence. Of confidence unearned, so much like the rich young men Erwin had seen when he was young: men who did not have to worry about money; men who knew just what to say; men who by their sheer bearing promised a life that women grasped for, with no further questions.

Erwin thought of his own father telling him to work hard at chores, to get calluses on his hands. "At Grandmother's house she'll ask to see," his father had said. "If you have calluses she'll be proud and give you treats." Checking little Erwin's palms, the old woman had beamed, and given him candy. He'd sat eating his candy, proud of his calluses and Grandmother's approval. He could not imagine the man in Sophia's photograph with calluses.

Leaving the photograph behind him, he found Geertruide and Herbert in the candle-lit dining-room. Sophia wore a plain white blouse, a charcoal woolen skirt and ivory cardigan. No matter how drably she dressed, she radiated something no woman ever had, as if she were defying him to dismiss her, even at her plainest.

"Hello," she said as if to an uncle. "I'm glad you agreed to join us. Children, say hello to Colonel Schell."

Each child said hello and looked down. Should he reply? What would a civilian say to them?

They sat. Sophia placed a dish on a trivet. "It's a boned rabbit, with mushroom and olive sauce." She must have seen his look of surprise. "From tins."

Erwin savored the first bite. "It's marvelous."

"Thank you. We don't have much to work with these days."

"You should make a list; it's permitted to fill a quartering family's pantry."

"Oh. It might look bad for the neighbors."

"Why would they know?"

"They wouldn't, necessarily. It's more the idea."

They were silent until Sophia said, "You know, there's one favor I might ask, if it's not too much."

"Anything, I'm sure."

"I've written my brother in Paris twice, with no reply. It's not like him to move suddenly without notifying me. I'm worried."

"There's been no trouble in Paris."

"I wonder if I sent another letter through the *Wehrmacht* post, would they handle it?"

"They would if I put it in my weekly pouch."

"Would you mind?"

"Just bring me the letter when you're ready."

The children quarreled, unshy of his presence. In ten minutes they had taken their last bites, and fidgeted until Geertruide asked, "May I be excused?"

"Yes," Sophia answered. "Go get ready for bed, and I'll come see you later."

Herbert looked up at his mother.

"You're excused, too. Go with Geertruide and get ready for bed."

The children hurried off.

Erwin looked at the candle. "It's clear you take considerable pleasure from them."

"I do. You know . . ." She broke off.

He looked up. "What?"

"Never mind."

"Say it. *Bitte.*"

"I sometimes think the way you raise your children is the most important thing in the world."

It was such a strange comment that Erwin had no idea how to reply. "Well . . . you seem an ideal mother."

Sophia laughed. "Thank you. I don't believe there is an ideal mother. Each one makes mistakes, learns from them and moves on."

Erwin looked at the tablecloth without answering. He had never heard a woman speak like this before.

Sophia continued in a low voice. "You know I love art, love to create. But it seems to me that child-raising, at least for those who think about it, is the ultimate creativity."

"Yes." He felt wooden.

"I suppose that sounds odd."

"Not at all." He felt he should say something more.

He felt a relief when Sophia went on. "Lieutenant Guse takes such an interest in my children."

"I've noticed. It's a great pleasure for him."

Sophia smiled at him kindly. "You're not so at ease with children, I think."

What a comment! "With children that age, perhaps not."

"Perhaps your own childhood was not so happy."

"No . . . I had a very happy childhood." What was happening? He heard his words come out quickly, with an edge. "A wonderful father."

Suddenly he was conscious of having exposed himself. The idea of this woman ten years younger, seeing his old painfulness and the odd feelings he could not describe, made him feel ridiculous. He barely maintained his composure.

"I should go."

"No coffee?"

What could he say to escape, without sounding too odd? He pushed his chair from the table, lifting to keep it from scraping the splendid carpet.

"Thank you, no. I have some paperwork. Dinner was splendid."

Sophia spoke as he walked away. "If you did have an unhappy childhood, it's no disgrace."

Unbearable, his soul laid open this way! He kept walking, and mumbled, "Thanks again."

Sophia smiled more kindly than anyone he could remember, and the fact that he needed kindness only made him feel more shame. "What are you trying to live up to?" she asked, still smiling. "You're only a person!"

Erwin closed the house's giant front door behind him and walked, nearly running, into the evening air, shaking his head as he thought what a fool he had made of himself. How could she understand the peculiar shame he had forgotten, this extraordinary being who thought herself "only a person," so beautiful and yet so free of vanity? It had always seemed to him that women used beauty as a kind of shield. Not this woman. Instead, Erwin felt as if his own hard shell were splintering against her soft unvanity.

What had he imagined he wanted from her? An image of himself, unchangeable in her mind? Erwin Schell wise, brave and selfless, branded forever in her consciousness.

Instead he had acted like an inmate in an insane asylum.

He wandered the river road for an hour.

Before bed, he lit his office lamp and composed a note.

> *I regret I was unable to stay longer at dinner. Captain Nagel returns today. I hope you'll let me reciprocate this evening. Seven o'clock in the dining room?*

He would give her the note first thing next morning.

Nagel wore a white apron. "Five more minutes."

Nagel's return made everything so natural again. To Erwin's relief, Sophia had not mentioned his strange departure last night.

"Thank you, Captain." Erwin turned to Sophia. "Will you change wines with dinner? He's serving trout."

"I'm not sure I have much to choose from."

"From my collection. I'll come right back."

He nearly skipped to the cellar, the alcoholic pleasure of the first glass mingling with the knowledge he was handling the evening much better.

He returned with a Chablis. "It's only cellar temperature, but I think you'll enjoy it."

He pulled the cork and filled two fresh glasses, almost toasted, "To Honor" as he did with his men, but realized how odd it must sound to a civilian, fumbled and quickly recovered, artful still from the alcohol of the first glass.

"To your health."

"To yours."

They both tasted. "You approve?"

"Very nice. A little chalky; a good one should be."

They sat and tasted the trout, browned in butter and parsley.

Sophia swallowed. "This is that special lake trout from Schwabia, isn't it?"

"Very good! What a German you might have been!"

He began to imagine Sophia secretly liked him.

Ten minutes later, exactly on schedule, the children asked to leave. Now he was alone with Sophia the second evening running. But tonight he would not take anything too seriously, would not ruin his second chance of a charming evening.

"Your glass is low." Erwin rose to refill it.

She laughed. "I've barely touched it. But thank you, only a little. There. Thanks."

Over the melodic bubbling Erwin said, "Tell me about your husband." As the words came out, he felt somehow confident that she might criticize the man in the photograph.

"Willem was a wonderful man to be married to."

"I'm sure he felt the same about you."

"I suppose."

Suppose! Did she doubt it? Something was evidently wrong between her and this small coin who had abandoned her. Erwin pressed a little. "Didn't he show you?"

As soon as the words left his lips, he wondered if he had offended. But Sophia paused, looked at him as if pondering his motive, and then apparently decided to be frank. She answered as if it were the most natural question in the world. "He didn't show his love in any particular way. Our marriage was beautiful because of what we had together: our house, our friends, our children. We had a wonderful life before the Germans came."

'Before the Germans came.' She had said it as if she had forgotten that he were German. Erwin swallowed a chalky sip of Chablis.

'What we had together.' So much left unsaid in that phrase; so much conspicuously missing.

Erwin challenged her with his eyes. "What he did is the real test. What sacrifices did he make for you?"

She looked confused. "I never asked him to sacrifice for me. Why would I?"

There she was, still defending this young nothing, but without conviction. Just words. Words like deceptive tips of icebergs, huge looming chunks of meaning beneath the surface. Beneath the words, surely she knew exactly what he meant.

He tried to sound objective, like an advisor. "If I were your husband, my love would be very clear."

Sophia pulled her hands apart and looked directly at him. "Colonel Schell, are you making a proposal?" She laughed, actually mocking him, but with eyes so friendly he felt no pain. Then he wondered if she felt sorry for him again, because she started to explain, as if to a simpleton cousin. "The man you walk down the aisle with, the man you hold your firstborn up to see -- you have a kind of communion together; he's part of your life on this Earth, like your parents or your children. Even when you know his faults, together you have something elemental, something you may never be able to create again."

'His faults.' Maybe this was the closest she would come to a full confession. Erwin pressed his advantage.

"One more question: how did this man get the good fortune to have this 'communion' with you?"

Sophia looked at him with tired eyes, as if she had answered the question a hundred times, if only to herself. "You should have known Willem Vaubin van Dordrecht in those days, at Leiden. So open, so approachable. Such a capacity for joy."

February, 1944

Nagel handed Erwin an envelope from Colonel Schussler. Erwin guessed its contents: too much time had passed with no word of Vogel and Strohn. Schussler's letter could only be a bitter confirmation.

> *Dear Erwin,*
>
> *I thought you would want to know. Vogel and Strohn died at Kursk. I'm sorry this news took so long. The Regiment notified their families immediately, but only I would have known to tell you. I just learned this week.*
>
> *Several of your Netherlanders died too; I do not have their names. Very sorry.*
>
> *Yours,*
> *Horst Schussler*

Erwin knew that General Langer could read his mood. He felt foolish as the General tried to cheer him up.

"Take the broader perspective. Most of Europe is still German. If the American landings fail, they will lose interest, and the Russians will fight alone again."

Erwin nodded and changed the subject. "Kessler and Zimmer don't leave for three more weeks, but since you are here I scheduled a farewell dinner tonight."

"Rommel will be lucky to have them defending the Channel."

"General, surely I should go now, too."

"You and Guse stay here. A single big victory will make the recruiting easy again."

General Langer scanned the bookshelves. "Well, what are we giving Kessler and Zimmer for their farewell supper?"

"Nagel's preparing a little veal."

"Wonderful. I brought some nice Rieslings."

"Nagel even has an American movie, from Spain."

General Langer raised his wineglass of geometric crystal. "To success at Normandy."

They all raised their glasses.

General Langer looked at Kessler and Zimmer. "You'll command *Osttruppen*: Rumanians, trained in Poland."

Nagel served a little salad with vinegar and thin-sliced rings of fresh onion.

Erwin looked at Kessler and Zimmer. "You'll probably meet Rommel."

"A second Erwin," Langer said.

"You know Rommel, don't you?"

"We write. He visits me on his trips home."

"We're told General Eisenhower will have overall command in Western Europe."

Nagel interrupted his serving. "Eisenhower. A good German name. No wonder he leads the Allies."

General Langer smiled. "It takes a German to fight a German."

In a darkened room they watched *Casablanca*, chuckling at the German *Kommandant's* sinister bombast.

After fifty minutes, the scenes stopped suddenly, and only the projector's broken light hit the screen. Nagel changed the sketchy film to a second roll, and they watched happily again.

At the end, they traded looks of appreciation.

"Play it, Sam."

"All the gin joints in the World. She came into mine."

"Very nice."

"Yes, very clever."

"Bogart's very special."

Kessler mouthed the nickname. "Bogey."

"The money such a movie must have cost: the actors, the equipment!"

"They make many movies. I hear Americans go to the cinema every weekend."

Erwin shook his head. "Making movies when they're at war. If they invest so much in movies, how can they possibly hope to win?"

Nagel's face darkened. "Or does it only show the Americans can produce on a scale past our imagining?"

March, 1944

Rudolph Schmidt was a full colonel of the SS, newly arrived in Rhenen. Colonel Schmidt looked like a retired heavyweight boxer who had gathered a layer of fat, pushing his cheeks up to form a malignant squint.

Today his manners were perfect as he came to pay his respects. He sat in the chair across Erwin's desk as if he would stay for hours. "It's the strangest place, Holland. All this trouble in Amsterdam. We had nothing comparable in the other Aryan cities: not Vienna, not Copenhagen, not Oslo. Anyway, we've cleared Amsterdam up. Now it's time for the smaller towns."

Erwin kept silent. This Colonel Schmidt reminded Erwin of Casablanca's caricature *Kommandant*, but untextured by the Casablanca character's comic softness.

"Rhenen," Schmidt went on. "An odd place, with its odd Cunera legend. Do you know it?"

"I think I've heard it told; I can't remember."

"The ridiculous thing is, here, with no serious resistance, the job is inexplicably unfinished. I stopped at the NSB office in town. These local Nazis! I said to them, 'A Jew sells publicly and still wears no star?' Guess how they answered!"

"How?"

"'He's the only Jew still in Rhenen,' they said. 'What's the point?'"

Erwin nodded, half hoping his nod would cue Schmidt to finish.

"Can you imagine? No feeling for History!"

Schmidt leaned close and touched Erwin's knee, German to German. "'Use patience,' I told myself. Aryans tend to be softhearted. This Jew is exploiting that weakness."

Colonel Schmidt continued without a reply, as if grateful for the audience of a peer. He spoke slowly and his tongue stuck to his dry lips at the beginning of each word. "Jews will wreck a nation, unless we have the stomach to inflict pain to protect it. Nobody likes Jews, but people shrink from the solution."

Colonel Schmidt rose and looked out the window, walked to the bookcase and scanned it, then turned again and spoke to Erwin as a soul-mate. "All these weaklings who dream of a better World, but do nothing unpleasant to achieve it! So different from you and me. I know all about you file. Almost no one rivals you. You and I grasp the question, and we know its answer: the Nation, the call of the blood!"

Colonel Schmidt rolled his eyes and softened his tone. "Maybe it's just a question of leadership. My first week here, I'll make a clear example."

Erwin tried to check his watch without being rude. Colonel Schmidt must have noticed, because he immediately announced, "Well! Thank you for your time. Come visit me at the NSB building in town, *bitte.*"

Nagel appeared from nowhere and escorted Colonel Schmidt out.

THE CHOOSING
Late March, 1944

Sophia led Herbert and Geertruide to Mr. Bloem's stall. Even now, it held curiosities from around the world: dried fruits from the Mediterranean, small carvings from African jungles, knick-knacks from China. Mr. Bloem's stall had always evoked romantic, faraway places. Today it also recalled better times, as she found herself smiling again at his quaint formality, at the way he wore his old suit with vest, coat and tie in any weather.

From the corner of her eye Sophia noticed a German officer and six soldiers approaching. Their uniforms were different from those of Colonel Schell's men. But on the leader's tight-fitting tunic, Sophia recognized a colonel's insignia and, as he neared, an SS badge. The other men were local NSB. Sophia reflexively slowed and let the colonel edge by.

The colonel spoke loudly to Mr. Bloem. *"Sie sind* Samuel Bloem?"

Mr. Bloem looked up with playful, inquisitive eyes.

Anxious that the old man's lack of German should not cause trouble, Sophia answered for him. *"Ja, er ist* Samuel Bloem."

The colonel ignored her. "You are a Jew, I believe."

Mr. Bloem nodded slowly, eyeing the colonel's face for purpose.

The colonel spoke as if to a truant schoolboy. "And yet you wear no star."

Mr. Bloem neither answered nor gestured.

Everything happened quickly. Two NSB hoisted Mr. Bloem by his armpits and pulled away his suit coat. They pulled his hands behind his back, popping the vest buttons, and cuffed his hands. Mr. Bloem looked amazed as they led him toward the church square. Sophia followed close behind, gripping each child by the hand, with townspeople trickling along after.

In the square stood a sturdy new post, with a bar across its top that made a thick 'T.' At the joint was fastened a hook, as large as a meat hook but blunt. The NSB helped Mr. Bloem step onto the chair in front, slowly and making allowance for his physical limits, like considerate train ushers helping an aging passenger. Then they tilted him forward and lifted his flabby arms behind and upward until the chain of his hand-cuffs fastened to the hook. They kicked the chair out from under and Mr. Bloem dropped heavily. His feet stopped short of the ground as the hook held his hands aloft, dislocating his shoulders. Sophia watched him squirm and kick, and heard snarls of pain grinding out of his mouth.

Sophia lurched to help, but another impulse pulled her quickly back, and she hurried the children away before they could see more. Her eyes burned as she pulled them along, unable to reply to their insistent questions.

Erwin heard the front door slam, and shoes clump across the floor. Without a knock, Sophia entered his office, sobbing, and gripped him. Was she saying that Nazis were killing someone in the square?

She spat out the words. "Is that a different line of authority too? *Verdomme!*"

Erwin stood in alarm. "What?"

"Follow me."

Was it the children? Adrenaline rocked him; he pushed her urgently before as they trotted to town and through Rhenen's western gate.

At the square Sophia was gone before he noticed. Erwin's eyes went to the old Jew on the post. Erwin shouldered through the crowd to find the old man still twitching. Ignoring the NSB guards, he unfastened the Jew's hands and caught him as he slumped. He checked for an expansion of the diaphragm, for heat or breath from the mouth. Nothing. No pulse.

He lifted the old Jew like a wounded soldier, over his shoulder, stumbling a little from the weight. The crowd did not make way as readily as he expected. "Shame!" someone said. Erwin looked up, but could not see who had said it. "Shame!" he heard again. He saw their looks of disgust; his face went red as he labored under the dead body. Finally he left the crowd on his way to the morgue on Hoogestraat.

"Shame!"

Rhenen's Burgemeester was well liked. Reformed Church but undogmatic, he was as affable with Catholics as with his fellow Protestants. He had always seemed slightly flattered when Sophia paid attention to him. But today the Burgemeester simply froze when Sophia slammed open his office door, her face quivering. "Do something!"

"What's the matter?"

Sophia pulled back the curtains and shouted "Look!"

"I don't see anything."

"They're torturing Mr. Bloem to death in the square! Where are the police?"

"Show me."

Sophia led the Burgemeester outside, to a spot where he could see Erwin lowering Bloem. The Burgemeester turned a little white, and she even wondered if he might faint.

Sophia's face was just inches from his. "It's been half an hour since the guards put him up there. Was I the first to come to you?"

The Burgemeester shook his head in disgust, and turned back into the *Gemeente Huis.* Following inside, Sophia asked, "What are you going to do?"

"Mevrouw Van Dordrecht, do you think these men will be stopped by policemen? This Jewish business is very serious to them."

Sophia leaned over his desk. "If you can't protect unarmed citizens, then why are you the Burgemeester?"

The Burgemeester lowered his voice and spoke to her as a friend. "Mevrouw Van Dordrecht, I think it's dangerous for you to make an issue of this."

"It would be dangerous for me not to make an issue of this."

The Burgemeester looked past her and called out, "Hello, Colonel Schmidt."

Now Sophia realized: the Burgemeester had been trying to warn her that the SS colonel was behind her. Too angry for caution, she turned and passed outside without returning the colonel's mumbled greeting. The buildings, people and clouds blurred as she walked.

That night Sophia held both children against her. Geertruide asked, "Mamma, is the story of David and Goliath true? Did David really kill a giant and save his people?"

Sophia looked at Geertruide's brown hair in the low light, and stroked it as she answered. "Many times, a weaker person or country has won through greater courage, greater cunning, or greater endurance. Holland rebelled from Spain when Spain was the most powerful nation on Earth. There have been many Goliaths, and many Davids. There will be more."

She held Geertruide close, rocking her as she had not done in months, and looked through the window into the night. "We can never know when some small David has seen enough, and is quietly loading his sling."

"For two nights in a row I can't sleep, thinking about that Frau Van Dordrecht," Colonel Schmidt confided. "Throwing a tantrum over a Jew's correction!"

Erwin held his words, and Colonel Schmidt quoted Hegel:

A single person, I need hardly say, is subordinate, and must dedicate himself to the ethical whole. Hence if the State claims life, he must surrender it.

Colonel Schmidt looked up. "Don't they see this? How could you have civilization without this principle?"

"Colonel, I . . . torturing an old man to death in public . . ." Erwin worried that if he spoke more directly, he would lose control of himself.

Colonel Schmidt looked at Erwin with bewilderment. "The *Führer* has explained the interests of the whole must set the limits and duties of the individual."

"I know the *Führer's* teachings." Erwin clipped his words to keep the anger inside his lips. "But I doubt the crucifixion of Jews is what the *Führer* imagined as the Heroism of Service."

Colonel Schmidt inhaled nasally, sucking back phlegm, and answered without reference to anything Erwin said. "The *Volk* is the organism. For this woman to act in isolation is to behave as a cancer cell. It's self-indulgent. It's . . . childish."

If only General Langer were here, Erwin thought. Langer would make a shrewd, unrebuttable answer and send this fanatic on his way.

Colonel Schmidt moaned. "These Netherlanders behave as if there were no consequences to behavior. This woman is like a rat crawling" -- he waived his arms -- "at leisure, in the open daylight."

The pugnacious face softened, as if leaving an opening for Erwin to agree. But Erwin kept silent; a minute passed with no exchange.

"It must have been a long time since she experienced pain," Schmidt continued. "Pain forces the acceptance of reality. Have you ever thought that people in pain are the only ones you can really trust? With pain there's no concealing."

Erwin avoided eye contact, polishing his revolver with a blackened white cloth.

"Imagine this woman separated from her children, wondering if they're still alive or whether she might have permission to see them. Imagine her face-down on the block in the SS basement, with screws driven into the flat ribs near her spine, threading against the exposed nerves. I can see her struggling to pull free, failing of course but still pulling until the chains tear her skin. Whimpering, moaning or screaming as her unconscious moves her because with this much pain there's no place for actual thought."

Erwin stood quickly, fumbled for something to say other than the unforgivable request simply to leave. But Colonel Schmidt finished before Erwin could think of anything.

"I can imagine her begging hysterically. With pain she would see how small and ridiculous she is."

Erwin gave the men a final Saturday off, before Zimmer and Kessler's departure for Normandy. Alone, he walked into Rhenen for a haircut. He took his time, as if it were still possible to purge the memory of local faces watching him carry the dead Jew, as if he might still see again the townsmen's distant but respectful nods.

He would speak with this Colonel Schmidt and suggest that the recruiting mission, such as it was, outranked any further demonstrations of power. That was the appropriate message. But that could wait until Monday.

"Good morning, Colonel Schell." The barber shop was freshly swept; Erwin could almost count the grains of dust under his boot soles crunching softly against the hard polished floor.

The barber arranged the cloth over Erwin's chest and knees, and spun the chair away from the door to face the mirrored wall. In the reflection Erwin watched the pedestrians outside, until he saw Sophia pass with the children. How would they spend the day? Maybe after the haircut he would walk in their direction.

In the square Sophia gazed into shop windows, until she saw Colonel Schmidt and a handful of NSB approaching, their eyes directly on her.

There is something pre-human in real terror, the terror a small animal feels when a predator has cornered it. Something in their look gave Sophia that animal terror, made her turn involuntarily away.

Colonel Schmidt spoke first. "Good morning, Frau Van Dordrecht. It's a beautiful day."

Sophia nodded with a correct smile.

"It's the strangest thing, but I hear a rumor you are Jewish. It seems impossible, married to a *jonkheer* -- can you help me understand?"

Was she really answering such a question? "I have no knowledge of any Jewish heritage whatsoever. Surely there are records."

She saw Colonel Schmidt listening carefully, as if looking for an opening.

"Thank you, you're perfectly right; that's the place to check." Colonel Schmidt looked at Herbert. "He's a beautiful boy; where's his father?"

Again Sophia found herself seeking to pacify this hideous man, to still the animal terror. "He was a doctor in the Army reserve, missing since the invasion."

Colonel Schmidt lifted Herbert and smiled like a father. Herbert squirmed.

"It's a shame: no one left to play with him the way fathers do." Schmidt tossed Herbert in the air to one of the NSB, who tossed him to another.

Herbert waved his arms. "Stop!"

"That's enough!" Sophia tried to laugh, as if a cordial ending were still possible, rather than show the anger she felt. But her voice betrayed her.

One of the NSB men sneered, "Oh, now! You don't want him to be a little priss!"

The other NSB laughed and threw Herbert higher, and the fear in his eyes was too much. The anger spoke through her. "Put him down!"

Even Geertruide shouted, "Stop it!"

Sophia lunged toward the man catching Herbert, but a large NSB gripped her painfully above the elbows and restrained her. Several townsmen, sturdy *boeren*, drew near, but she saw their faces tighten as they mastered the impulse to intervene, and she despaired.

Then one, Mr. Brinksma with the hardware store, stepped in suddenly and caught Herbert as if joining in the game, but placed Herbert on the ground. The largest NSB man grabbed Brinksma by the belt and collar and rammed his face into the brick wall of the church. The NSB man lifted Herbert again and returned him to the ring of NSB.

Sophia was reduced to helpless fury, like a jay defending her hatchling against a viper, unable to do more than make noise.

Erwin paid the barber a guilder and tipped him a *kwartje*. With irritation he noticed a scuffle down Hoogestraat, disturbing the Saturday calm. Then he recognized Herbert, tossed from man to man, and saw Sophia hysterical and restrained. He quickened to a trot, and gripped his sword handle.

Reinhard Guse reached them first.

Hurrying toward them, Erwin saw it all. Guse's physical difference from the NSB men was striking; Guse was a head taller, and moved like an athlete. Like a colt which can barely keep its balance, as its speed surpasses its own expectation when it first stretches its young legs to run, so the force of Guse's movements surprised everyone looking. Kicking the stomach of the man waiting to catch the boy, Guse sent the man backward all the way to the church wall, his body folded with the air gone from his lungs and his lowest ribs almost certainly broken. Guse caught Herbert and placed him against Sophia.

The man holding Sophia let go and faced Guse. Without waiting for the man to act, Guse smashed the ball of his hand between the man's lips and nose; the man crumpled without breaking his own fall.

Swearing, another NSB stepped toward Guse from the right and behind. In a swift, continuous back-hand, Guse smoothed his sword from its scabbard, ramming the haft into the attacker's cheek. The man spun a full circle from the blow's centrifugal force, his face seeming to pull the rest of his body along before he fell.

In a ring formed by the remaining attackers, Guse flashed the sword in a figure-eight, in a swift blur like an airplane propeller, challenging them to draw a weapon, breathing hard in his fury.

Erwin's hand moved from his own sword to clutch his *Luger* instead. "*Was ist das? Was ist das?*" It came out like a command instead of a question. "Put away your sword!"

In Guse's anger, Erwin was the one man who could speak to him this way and be obeyed. Still uncertain what might happen,

Erwin faced Schmidt. "I'm arresting this man from my squadron. Lieutenant," he said to Guse, "Wait in my office. Go."

Guse paused. Suddenly he turned and walked toward the western gate. Sophia carried Herbert away with Geertruide close behind.

Facing Colonel Schmidt, Erwin tried to maintain his self-control. "Is that all your NSB can do? Bully civilians?"

Colonel Schmidt looked at Erwin with absolute surprise. "Does your superior know you're doing this?" It seemed less a challenge than a genuine bewilderment, as if Erwin had sprouted wings.

"If my superior were here, this would never have happened! You'd never dare to act like street thugs in the presence of General Langer."

Erwin felt himself out of control. He saw Colonel Schmidt now grow calm again, and knew that his own lack of composure only gave confidence to his enemy.

"Colonel Schell, you seem to have a special relationship to this woman. Have you considered the possibility she's an enemy of your country?"

"What's your evidence?" Erwin hissed the words.

Schmidt kept quiet.

"Show me your evidence!"

Schmidt's lip quivered almost imperceptibly. "Be careful, Colonel Schell, extremely careful. I'm certain our *Führer* would not approve of your lieutenant's behavior. Nor of your own."

One NSB man took a step after Guse, but stopped at the sound of Erwin slipping the safety catch of his *Luger*. Their eyes met and held. Erwin wondered whether he could master his anger. If he fought these men, there was no question who would prevail. These were not Myrmidons, or Colonel Schussler. With these he was like a lion among hyenas; a greater number uninjured might threaten him, but not this damaged little group. Erwin felt the adrenaline renew him. Each movement reaffirmed that old, fluid feeling, the perfect confidence of his own physical skills. Schmidt spoke again. "You understand there's no question of your lieutenant going free. By military law he's my responsibility. I expect to hear from you tomorrow."

Erwin reflected. With the correct body rotation, his elbow in Schmidt's unprepared ribs would crack them at least, and likely cave them into the lungs. How could NSB retaliate? Only Schmidt rivaled Erwin's authority; killing him here and now would be the simplest thing.

Instead Erwin turned and walked toward the western gate.

Outside the city wall he overtook Sophia and the children. He reached to take Herbert from Sophia's arms. "Thank you," she gasped. "My heart's still pounding; it feels too large for my ribs to hold it."

Erwin forced Herbert to meet his gaze. "Look at me," he said. "Those men frightened you, didn't they?"

Herbert shook his head no, as tears ran down his cheeks.

"Herbert, these men are cowards who temporarily have some authority. Real National Socialists are very different. These will not hurt you, I promise."

Herbert still did not react. Erwin lowered his voice. "Herbert, I will not let anything bad happen to you. Do you understand?"

Herbert nodded.

Erwin looked at Sophia, to see that she understood how different he was from these men. But today Sophia offered him no reflection of himself. Sophia looked tired and beaten.

Sophia watched Guse set a mattress in the brick shed that would be his makeshift jail. Zimmer and Kessler brought books and candles. For lack of any better gesture, Sophia carried out half a cold roasted chicken on a cracked china plate. After re-bolting the door, she spoke through the small window. "You're in trouble for my sake."

Guse did not reply.

Sophia wiped her eyes. "I've never felt so helpless. I don't know what might have happened, without you."

But Guse's emotions heated and cooled to other cadences now than Sophia's voice. He looked past her at the clouding sky. "Those men are criminals, not National Socialists. They disgrace me." Guse pounded the door so hard it seemed about to break open. He raked a row of clay flowerpots from a wooden shelf, shattering them on the brick floor.

Sophia stayed a minute longer. Then, unsure what else to say, she stepped toward the house. On the way she met Erwin, coming to secure the lock.

"What will happen?" she asked.

He looked at the ground. "The SS will insist on taking custody, but . . . Tomorrow I can reach General Langer -- he'll know what to do."

He studied Sophia's eyes. "Get some rest. Nagel will arrange things."

"The Farm Inspector's coming before dinner."

"The Farm Inspector! I'll tell him to come another time."

Sophia touched his elbows. "No!" Then she softened. "He has his obligations too, and he's an honest man. I don't want to delay him."

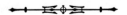

"I think we have everything we need. Thank you for the information."

The Farm Inspector was always so ... calculating. In his presence, any problem seemed solvable.

"You're confident?" she asked.

"We're ready."

"I'm ready too."

"You don't have to do this," he said as quietly as a confessor. "You made your contribution stealing the Poland letter for us to distribute."

"Others have done so much more. It's my turn."

"Others had less to risk. Think of your children."

"I am."

A lamp burned low in Erwin's bedroom.

"Erwin." Sophia crossed his threshold.

Erwin put down his reading and stood. How must his cluttered room look to her! "Have you ever called me 'Erwin' before?"

Sophia thrust her soft body against him casually, as if for the hundredth time; from her shining black hair a few strays touched his chin. He patted her back, pretending he knew what to do, hoping his thrill was invisible.

Her voice pulsed through her breasts against his ribs. "I know you're in a difficult situation."

"Yes, I am. But General Langer will think of a solution."

Tears flowed down Sophia's hot cheeks. Erwin found that her emotion strangely calmed him.

"What happened today terrified me," she said. "I was lucky Lieutenant Guse was near." Her voice cracked as she finished.

It suddenly occurred to him that Sophia was lonely beyond any imagining. For the first time, he grasped that she needed a friend, that it was not a matter of saying the correct thing or impressing her, but only of holding her, accepting her. Had she never needed him before, or was it only that he had never seen it?

He made a fish-mouth with his lips and stared over Sophia's head. Sophia held him tighter, so that his chest touched the soft points of her shoulders. Somehow Erwin knew she was ready to make love to him here and now.

But tonight he would not. As hungrily as he wanted her, he wanted her not in defeat, but at the height of her power and consciousness, when she was proud and remarkable, as she had been only weeks before.

He led her to the sofa. "Please sit down."

From the closet he pulled a thick blanket and draped it over her knees, then blew out the candle and turned off the lamp. Sitting, he pulled her near and rocked her. He wrapped the blanket around Sophia, shielding her from the chill and from his own touch, and held her until she fell asleep in his arms.

At daylight she woke, alone on Erwin's sofa, to the sound of shouting. She stepped outside into the chill. Across the canal stood Erwin, Nagel, Zimmer and Kessler at the shed's open door. Guse was gone.

Erwin's voice choked as they strutted toward the house. "These criminals!" She saw him snarl. "Get your weapons; we leave in five minutes!"

Erwin's group trotted down the brick street in full combat gear. Townsmen shuffled in alarm from their path, until the group reached the NSB office at the corner of Stationsweg and Hoogestraat.

The curtains there were drawn. Nagel, Zimmer and Kessler separated into covering positions, a rifle sight on each window. Erwin stepped to the door and knocked. He knocked again. As a final prelude to kicking in the door, he twisted the doorknob, but it opened easily and he nearly stumbled inside.

Through the windows frail sunbeams lit the interior. Erwin called out a mild *"Achtung"*, but the only reply was his echo. He toured the vacant ground floor, then stepped up the staircase. A bustle behind and downstairs told him Nagel and the others had followed him in.

At the stair top, he found Colonel Schmidt and his men in their sleeping clothes, strewn like dolls on wide pools of blood, heads bludgeoned and throats severed. Erwin crossed through the upstairs until he was sure that Guse was not one of the bodies. Then he returned to Colonel Schmidt, where a pair of flies buzzed over the bluing lips. Touching Colonel Schmidt's body, Erwin found it cold, dead for hours. On the floor he found an olive felt cap with a golden shield, the cap of the Netherlander he had pardoned months before.

On the lawn Sophia saw Erwin and the others leading the Dutch turncoat, the one they had freed months ago. Now the man's face was more shaken and forlorn than ever. After Erwin's group led him inside, Sophia waited in the cold and watched.

After ten minutes Kessler and Zimmer brought the man back outside. His face was so pale she could see his green veins. He resisted only an instant, then let the soldiers tug him toward the woods and out of sight. Sophia heard a gunshot.

Erwin closed the door behind him and stepped toward her. "Once we arrested this man for spying. I let him choose: be shot or work for Germany. He chose to work for us. But this morning I found every man in the NSB office dead, with this man's cap on the floor."

She hardly listened. "Was Lieutenant Guse there?"

"No. That's another factor: did this assassin kill Guse unarmed in the shed? Or did he free Guse, recruit him for the murder and then put him in hiding? This man of course claimed he had nothing to do with it, said his cap was there because his house had been burglarized."

Sophia spoke slowly, too. "You're sure this man was guilty?"

"We went to his house and found a shirt still wet with blood. I suppose the burglar put the bloody shirt there, too! Unbelievable."

She buried her face in Erwin's tunic to hide her relief. The Farm Inspector's group had succeeded beyond any hope: freed Guse, surprised Colonel Schmidt and the NSB, burglarized the turncoat's house as she had suggested, stolen his cap and planted the blood-stained shirt. She had scarcely dared believe they could accomplish it.

At Sophia's suggestion, the Farm Inspector had replaced the normal reprisal list in the NSB's files, substituting a fabricated list of men they thought were secret collaborators. If the fake reprisal list worked, the whole affair would drastically change the momentum in the underground war. Sophia looked at Erwin again. "Won't Schmidt's killing bring reprisals?"

"This man should have considered that before he acted." His voice quieted. "I found the reprisal list in the NSB files, and saw hand-written notes beside the names; I'm sure they're suspected saboteurs. I'll arrest them and turn them over to the military police in Arnhem for a firing squad."

Incredible, she thought. The idea had seemed almost too ambitious, but ...

Erwin went on. "The only question now is: where the hell is Guse?"

In the greenhouse Sophia painted yellow flowers. Somehow she was not surprised when she heard Erwin's footsteps on the cement floor.

"Nice to see you painting again."

"Did you send my letter?"

"I sent it. Let me think, it must have been six weeks ago or more."

"I've gotten no reply."

"If it went in the *Wehrmacht* mail, then it reached him."

Five minutes passed as Erwin watched. "What color is scarcest?"

"Red," she answered without looking up. "Red paints are the scarcest. They were always expensive, and now impossible to find."

"Maybe I'll find you some. I'm going to see General Langer about the Schmidt problem. I may make a little detour to Cologne. Red, you say, just ordinary red?"

"Like the red in a red wagon, or the red in a rose, either one. It stops me painting apples and red flowers, or even orange things. I doubt you'll find any."

On Saturday Erwin invited Sophia to his office. "I have a surprise for you."

Sophia smiled. "I can't imagine what."

Erwin lifted a long wooden box from his shelf, then opened it to reveal two long rows of paint tubes. "Two kinds of red," he said. "The red of a rose, and the red of red wagons."

Sophia took one of the metallic tubes in her fingers. "This must have cost you a year's salary."

"Much more; you overestimate *Wehrmacht* pay."

Sophia eyed the gray sleeves and sinewy hands holding the box. A consciousness lifted her, of a man living selflessly in relation to her, as a parent does for a child. A kaleidoscope of emotions rushed to her face like blood: the most elemental sensations of security and attachment.

It was not a kind of love she had conditioned herself to feel, fixated like every girl at Leiden on the handsome young men like schools of herring after food, flashing their brilliant skins in simultaneity. None of them could have explained why they felt the way they did. None would ever have felt anything for a forty-year-old in gray *Wehrmacht* wool and medals.

That was so long ago. From this man she felt unqualified love. With Erwin she saw the enchanting vision, an escape from aloneness. Maybe not alone after all. Not, at least, if she chose.

Suddenly it seemed imperative to prolong this feeling, to keep him near. She took the box from his hands and laid it on his desk, then kissed his face and neck.

Later, Erwin would not recall whether he led Sophia or she led him into the bedroom. But it was Sophia who drew the curtains.

Never had Erwin felt so exposed, or such reward in the exposure. He touched and kissed her breasts, her stomach, the spot where her thigh met her abdomen. His head spun and he felt warm, warmer even than her delightful skin which sprang in response to his touch, revealing her to him in ways language never had. The hardly-imagined dream was suddenly a reality.

Each day her attention still surprised and thrilled him. In the night's quiet, long after the children were asleep, she came. He treasured the feel of his legs pressed against hers, the way her soft skin warmed his own. Many times he lay awake against her, reflecting how late in life he had found this sacrament.

THE STRANGEST PEOPLE IN THE WORLD
March, 1944

At the corrugated tin building Willem Vaubin van Dordrecht hesitated, then knocked.

"What is it?" the voice inside was throaty. Opening the door, Willem saw a black-haired man pouring condensed milk into a stained coffee mug. The man held out his hand to shake, without moving closer, or interrupting the pouring. "Captain Edward Brady, U.S. Army."

The American Captain Brady stood six feet tall, with narrow shoulders that drooped as if sagging from the weight of his little beer belly. His black hair had receded all the way across the top of his head. Willem stepped close and shook Brady's hand; then Brady returned to sit behind his desk.

"Sit down," Brady gestured to the metal chair, next to a set of shelves leaning unassembled against the desk. Against the stack of shelving lay a pile of books. The spine on the top book read *Amphibious Doctrines.*

Brady unfolded a paper and read silently. His eyes were still on the paper when he finally spoke. "Dr. Willem Vaubin van Dordrecht."

"That's right."

"We're going into a damned hot kitchen. You had any combat experience?"

"It doesn't matter."

Brady squinted as if the sun were in his eyes. "Doesn't matter."

Willem almost told the story of the May days of 1940, when his unit had retreated across Holland, when he had never seen an enemy soldier, or fired his weapon. Instead he said, "I worked convoy surgery in the North Atlantic for twenty-seven months."

Brady screwed one eye in a half-wink, plainly wondering what convoy duty must be like. "This is a volunteer unit, assigned a fortified bunker. Did someone tell you that?"

Willem wondered how to express himself. "In April, 1940, I was a village doctor. In the May days I was a reserve captain in the Army of the Netherlands. After we evacuated to England, I wore a British military doctor's khaki. When the bombing slowed, I joined the convoys. As I eat, drink and breathe, every atom in every cell of my body has changed since then; there's no physical fact that defines me. There's only one continuity." Willem tapped his temple. "Here, in the mind; my purpose. Getting home to my family is the only thread connecting my past and my present and my future. So you won't talk me out of landing because of danger."

Brady wrote a note in a tiny spiral notebook, then looked up at Willem.

"You're a surgeon?"

"Yes."

"What languages?"

"Dutch, German, English, French, in that order. Very good German. Enough French to communicate, not enough to be mistaken for a Frenchman."

Brady pushed his chair back. "Well, you may not be a lot greener than the rest of my men. I left my old company in Italy to form a new one with men from other units. We've got to train like hell." Brady looked at the floor and seemed to forget about Willem for a minute, then rediscovered him. "Anyway, meet me here tomorrow morning at six. We'll walk over together to meet Sergeant Haggerty's squad."

"Six o'clock." Willem repeated as he rose to leave.

Brady squinted at the notebook. "Wait, one more thing."

Willem sat again. "What's that?"

"You evidently have connections. You may think those connections can keep you in this unit whether I want you or not. But you're wrong. We can't have anyone on this team who's going to fuck it up. My C.O. asked for an evaluation one month into this."

"What are you going to evaluate?"

"Well, I made a note when you were talking. I got the impression you're anxious to get home. Fair enough. But these men are real people, not toy soldiers. If you think they're just your ride home, they're going to sense it, and it's going to fuck up the whole team."

When Willem said nothing, the American leaned forward. "Do you have any idea what makes men fight?"

Willem shifted sideways. "Yes, I think I do. I want to fight because someone invaded my country and stole my property. Frankly speaking, I think I understand that better than you do."

"I didn't say 'want to fight.' Men that think they 'want to fight' are everywhere. That doesn't mean you will, once you're there. Try again. What do you think makes men actually fight, when the enemy's in killing range, when every instinct's telling you to run like hell?"

"I don't know."

"From what I've seen, it's his sense that if he leaves, he's abandoning men he's committed to. And the security that the other man won't abandon him."

Brady and Willem looked at each other.

"By the time we leave, the men will either believe that about you or they won't. And if they don't, then having you in the unit will just screw it up."

Brady stood and they shook hands coldly.

The next morning, Willem was back at Brady's tin lodge at a quarter to six. One minute before the hour, Brady stepped out onto the gravel and greeted Willem cheerfully. They walked in the ungenerous English dawn, past huts and tents to the parade ground where a group of enlisted men already sat. The gravel still crunched under the soles of Brady's walking feet as he interrupted their chat.

"Good morning, glories. I'm Edward Brady."

No one answered. Brady moved his gaze slowly from face to face.

"Let me start with a question. How many think your parents want a dead war hero instead of a son? Raise your hands."

Everyone shifted without speaking.

"OK. Then we understand each other. Any of you wants to become a war hero, let me know and I'll move you to another outfit. In any company I command, staying alive is rule number one."

"Look at Mad Jack here." Brady pointed to the squad sergeant, a squatty man with a misshapen face. "Mad Jack was a sergeant before the war started, and he's still not promoted. That tells you my lieutenants aren't getting killed. In fact, I have forbidden them all to get killed. I forbid each of you to get killed, too."

Willem saw a row of blank faces, saw Brady study the men for looks of comprehension.

"Anyone here ever been in combat?"

The men looked at the ground and Brady knelt close. "Let me tell you about real combat. You'll know you're in it when the ground starts exploding all around you, and men next to you start falling from bullets you can't see. It will scare you almost out of your mind. The second or third or fourth time, it will still scare you almost out of your mind. When it stops scaring you, let me know and I'll send you home because I'll know you're crazy.

"Anyway, rule number two is not to go out of your mind. The secret is knowing what to do when you're scared almost out of your mind. That's what an army is: a group of men who still function when they're scared half to death. Anything else is just a mob."

Brady lowered his voice. "The enemy wants you to turn into a mob, so it's easy to kill you. We want to just keep on being an army, and turn *them* into a mob and kill them.

"Now, one way to become a mob is to run. That's the natural reaction. But it's when you're running, when your back is to the enemy, that you're defenseless. Running is usually fatal. When we fight, the kill zone may be a mile deep and ten miles wide. Can you even imagine that? There really is no place *to* run. There's really no safe place until you've killed the Germans. The most dangerous thing will be to hang back.

"Remember all this when you start to practice the crazy things that Mad Jack is going to make you do. If you master your training, you have a pretty good chance of coming home alive to your mothers and fathers."

Brady looked around. "OK. Let's get your names and where you're from."

"Ron Ichinowski. Detroit."

"You look like Joe DiMaggio."

"That's what everyone says, Sir. My mother says Joe DiMaggio but goofier lips."

Brady turned to the next man, a boyish face with auburn hair, just finishing a yawn.

"Ryan Gilker. Chicago."

"They call you Red?"

"Not really, Sir."

Brady's gaze moved to the next soldier.

"Anthony Carbone. New York."

"Where in New York?"

"New York, New York."

"OK. Who's next?"

A man with enormous shoulders said, "John Stringer. Akron, Ohio."

Willem barely heard a soft-spoken man with black hair and dark skin. "John Hightower. Muldrow, Oklahoma."

"James Douglass. Coffeyville, Kansas."

"Robert Glass. Duluth." Willem could hardly look at Glass's pimply face.

"Minnesota?"

"Right."

"Forrest Hall. Martin, Tennessee."

"Stephen Green. Omaha, Nebraska."

"Green? I guess you're ready to shoot some Nazis."

"I hope everyone here is, Sir."

"Who's next? What about you, Private?"

"Howard Lindell. But people call me 'Buster.' San Angelo, Texas."

"OK. This is Captain Willem van Dordrecht. He's a doctor attached to the medical battalion, but he'll train and land with your squad. He actually wants to fight in squad. Don't ask me why. The Germans threw the good doctor out of Holland four years ago and he says he's ready to go back. Speaks ten languages. Going to land with us, interpret, and save all your lives when you forget what Mad Jack's going to teach you."

Brady scanned their faces again. "That's it. Dismissed."

Brady rose from his crouch and walked away, leaving Willem with the men.

The first to walk over was Ichinowski, the man who had said he had goofy lips. "I'm a Polack. You don't look Dutch."

"How'd you expect a Dutchman to look?"

"I don't know. But you look pretty normal."

Willem lost track of the jokes as soon as they began. "Ten languages! The doctor's a cunning linguist. He can't wait to get to France."

"Dr. Van Dordrecht, Dr. V.D.!"

"The V.D. Doctor!"

"Must be some reason they put the V.D. Doctor in our squad. They're sendin' us to Paris!"

After sunset, Willem brushed his teeth by the faucet and bowl outside the latrine. He let the cold water mix with the powder on his toothbrush, sat on an overturned crate and tasted the grainy, sweet stringent.

"Hey, Buddy! You can't sit there! This is the goddamned Army!"

Willem looked up and saw a soldier walking fast: was it one of the men he had met that morning, Ichinowski? The man moved quickly away before Willem could react.

Through the latrine's cinderblock walls, Willem heard a man sing in a nasal drawl, yodeling between the verses:

> *If you don't want me, Mama*
> *You sure don't have to stall.*
> *If you don't want me, Mama*
> *You sure don't have to stall.*
> *'Cause I can git more women*
> *Than a passenjo train can haul.*
>
> *I'm going to buy me a shotgun*
> *With a great long shiny barrel.*
> *I'm going to buy me a shotgun*
> *With a great long shiny barrel.*
> *I'm going to shoot that rounder*
> *That stole away my ga-a-a-a-al.*

The latrine door slammed and a tall man emerged, blondish like Willem but taller and thinner, with hard shoulders, narrow eyes and a big nose.

"You're the Dutchman, aren't you?"

"I am."

The man put out his hand. "Buster Lindell. We met this morning."

Brady skipped the squad's first day of training.

"Line up!" Mad Jack Haggerty, his belly given shape by his tight fatigue shirt, walked up and down the line, frowning and rolling his eyes. "I can tell already you're gonna embarrass me."

Mad Jack shook his head. "Oh, well. Let's start with a march. Maybe you can at least handle that."

Mad Jack punctuated the march with strange cadences, a tobacco plug in his cheek, too much tobacco for his words to be understood, and it seemed as if he were mastering some speech impediment.

"What's he saying?" Willem asked Lindell.

Lindell spoke along with Mad Jack, just loud enough for Willem to hear:

> *Left, right, it's hard but it's fair.*
> *You had a good home but you wouldn't stay there.*

"Be quat!" Without stopping the march, Mad Jack walked up to Lindell and shouted in his ear. "I'm goan fire you."

Lindell waited till Haggerty filtered away, then spoke softly. "Fire me!" He snorted. "As if being fired from the Army was somethin' horrible."

When Mad Jack eventually stopped his cadence, Lindell began to sing, beginning so low that only Willem could hear.

> *I'm going to California, where they sleep out every night.*
> *I'm going to California, where they sleep out every night.*
> *I'm leavin' you, Mama, 'cause you know you don't treat me right.*

The volume grew with every verse until Willem was sure even Mad Jack could hear it, but now Mad Jack seemed no longer to care about keeping Lindell quat.

> *I don't understand how come you treat me like you do.*
> *I can't understand what makes you treat me like you do.*
> *If you don't want me, Mama, it's a cinch I don't want you.*

Lindell turned to Willem as they marched. "People in Holland ever listen to The Legendary Jimmy Rodgers?"

"Who?"

"Jimmy Rodgers."

"I'm afraid not."

Lindell faced ahead. "Unbelievable. Well, then, I'll bring the music of Jimmy Rodgers to Europe."

Willem's feet began to blister. It didn't matter. Not the blisters, not the Legendary Jimmy Rogers, not Mad Jack Haggerty, nothing at all could disturb him, looking down the drab green of his fatigue pants, pants of serge he had not worn since 1940, pants that meant the journey home was finally coming.

"Mail call!"

The men sprang into a circle around Lieutenant Gerber, their faces like lost children waiting for their parents.

"Hightower!"

Hightower grasped a faded lavender envelope and stepped away, oblivious to the others crowding Lieutenant Gerber.

"Ichinowski!"

Ichinowski swiped the envelope from Gerber's hand. Gerber glared back but Ichinowski was already walking away with his prize.

"Slow down," Gerber called to him. "Here's another one."

Ichinowski showed no sign of slowing until Stringer echoed the call. "Icky-boy!"

Ichinowski turned, still only half looking up from his letter. Gerber said, "You've got another one."

Finally Ichinowski understood, and came back through the impatient men. Ichinowski reached up for his second letter, but Gerber held it back. Ichinowski held out his hand politely, and finally Gerber gave it to him.

"Douglass! . . . Gilker! . . . Hall!"

Soon each man held a letter, some two or three, till only Gerber and the empty-handed Willem remained. Gerber looked at Willem, but said nothing.

Lindell looked up from his mail and called to Willem. "Get this," Lindell began. "Brother Joe's killin' my calves."

Willem stepped a little nearer and Lindell read aloud.

Dear Buster

> *You're not going to like this, but another one of your two-month-olds died of scours, for a grand total now of three. I called the vet over to see calves one and two and lo and behold we came across calf number three, under the stickler tree. The fur was gone from his bewtocks, and maggots were eating him while he still lived. I felt terrible, make no mistake. Anyway, we'll get this figured out before you come home.*

Lindell shook his head. "Joe can rodeo but you CAN NOT leave him in charge of calves."

Douglass called. "Hey Willem! Want to see a picture of my family?"

Douglass held up a photograph of a father with no expression, and an aging woman with sharp, intelligent eyes.

Douglass read aloud from a feminine cursive.

Dear James

Not much news over here, except that your collie

Douglass interrupted his reading, "my dog's name is Patch, and she still calls him 'my collie.'"

Your collie came home snake-bit. Her paw

Douglass interrupted himself again. "It's a male, but she calls him a 'her' as a mark of affection."

Her paw swelled up the size of a boxing glove and she crawled under the house for four days. I put food and water out but she would not touch the food. The fifth day, she crawled out as good as new.

A happy smile spread over Douglass' face.

These men, Willem thought to himself. He was a charity case, without the precious currency of letters. They shared their wealth as best they could, artfully, without demeaning him.

In the first aid tent, Ryan Gilker winced as Willem lanced his boil.

"How long you had this?"

"Nearly a week. I thought it would go away."

Willem clucked with the side of his lips. "Easy to get these in the Army. Hard to keep as clean as you can at home."

Willem ignored Gilker's stare and poked at the boil. Finally Gilker spoke. "You remind me of the priests who taught me in high school."

Willem laughed without smiling. "In Holland, that would be no compliment."

"I meant it as one. They were really my, uh, mentors for a while."

Willem collected the boil's ooze. "Why do I remind you of them?"

"Not sure." Gilker paused. "I guess the word might be serene. Not caught up in little things."

Willem laughed without smiling again. He threw away the cotton swab and dosed another with alcohol.

Gilker continued, "I was their fair-haired boy: valedictorian, state champ in the eight-eighty. They all thought I'd become one of them."

"A priest?"

"I'm pretty sure they expected it."

"What happened?"

"Ow!" Gilker jumped. "Well, I stopped believing in God, for one thing. Have you ever known you disappointed someone who really invested in you? They weren't angry, just . . . pained might be the word. They'd always been so, so nice to me. But what else could I do? Lie to them?"

Willem cleansed a little longer. "What do you believe in now?"

"Reason. Individuality. Freedom."

"You think the priests didn't?"

"They believe in faith, service, and sacrifice, actually the opposites of what I believe in."

Gilker looked at the tent ceiling, as if trying to remember. "'I swear, upon the altar of my conscience, implacable hostility toward every form of tyranny over the mind of man.' Thomas Jefferson. I think that's right. Anyway, even if it's wrong, it says it pretty well. Sure, they teach it: Boston Tea Party, Continental Congress. But they don't understand it. To them, your country is one more thing to sacrifice yourself to."

Odd words from one so boyish, Gilker with his shining eyes, the red hairlets that stopped before his ears without becoming whiskers.

"Well," Willem said. "That ought to heal in a couple of days. Come back if it doesn't."

Haggerty studied the men in line; then from his misshapen mouth came a quiet benediction. "This is our last day in squad. Starting tomorrow we train in battalion. Don't embarrass me."

They scaled low cliffs with ropes and ladders, mock Germans pushing the ladders back or cutting the ropes, or touching the climbers with wooden bayonets. Mad Jack shouted, "Germans will conquer the World, with only you turtledoves in their way."

Stephen Green neared the top when a mock German pushed his ladder back. The mock German groaned, "Oh, shit!" as he saw the distance Green fell. Green landed hard, grimaced and held his right shoulder.

Willem was the first to trot over and check the injury. "Dislocated. Can you walk?"

Rising, Green turned whitish, as if he might faint. Willem supported him all the way to the medical tent. Green slid onto the exam table and removed his shirt, exposing a slender neck chain with his dog-tags and a Star of David.

Green winced as Willem moved the arm, testing the injury.

"You really speak ten languages?"

Willem stopped. "No, what made you think I did?"

"When Brady introduced you the first day, that's what he said."

Remembering, Willem snorted. "I don't know why he said that. Actually, I speak four."

"That's amazing. No one in America can do that."

Green eyed the medical instruments around the tent. "My parents wanted me to be a doctor."

"Why didn't you?"

"In college I thought I wanted to be a writer." Green glanced up at Willem, then cast down his eyes down and made a pinched smile that quickly left.

"What kind of writer?"

"Something that would last. I read Homer, Shakespeare, and all the great novelists. I used to wonder what made a great writer better than a good writer."

Green made the pinched smile again, then became silent until Willem spoke. "I'm putting your arm in a sling. Put some ice on it the first twenty-four hours. After that, heat. You should be able to get a hot-water bottle in the commissary. Come back to me if you can't."

As Willem wrapped the arm, Green continued. "When I actually tried to write something big, something on the scale of a Shakespeare, a Cervantes, or even a Wodehouse as I slowly got less ambitious, I realized I had nothing to say. I was good at putting words on paper, but what was my story? So journalism seemed the second best thing; maybe later in life I'd have a story. I wrote the papers in Kansas City, Chicago and St. Paul for a summer job, but got drafted."

"Do you have any idea what made you want to write?"

"I don't know." Green laughed through his nose. "That's what I wonder: am I another Virgil? Or just an oddball?"

"Only one way to find out, I guess."

"That's true."

Willem organized the medical instruments, but Green ignored his cue to leave. Willem wondered if the boy had spoken to anyone this way since leaving home.

They crawled below machine gun level, bringing up Bangalore torpedoes, blowing through barbed wire, moving through the openings fast and low. They crossed minefields on their stomachs, using extended rods to trip the mines. Willem and the other men were reaching the point where each could do his own job or the next man's automatically, without having to think consciously of the steps.

Mad Jack was never satisfied. "I wish I was a German, because if you young ladies are the best America can do, they'll have an easy time. How I wish I was a German, fighting you."

Lieutenant Gerber stopped by the barracks after exercises. "Willem. Captain Brady wants to see you."

Willem still breathed hard from the drill, mud still drying on his face. "Fine. I'll be there in minute."

Standing in the chilly shower, Willem wondered what Brady wanted.

At the corrugated tin building, he found Brady in the entry room. Brady extended a hand. "Let's go for a beer."

They walked to the tented beer hall and found a corner table. Brady tapped the tabletop and looked for a waiter. "Well, is Mad Jack turning you into a soldier?"

"I guess you never know until we land."

A waiter brought two beers in dimpled goblets. Brady took a drink from the frosted rim and seemed to relish the thin lager, but American beer was the worst Willem had ever tasted.

Willem spoke again. "Sergeant Haggerty never seems to be satisfied."

Brady laughed and stopped himself. "Haggerty." He laughed again. "Haggerty's the biggest bull-shitter in the U.S. Army."

Brady laughed again. "But he can train people. He's the most practical man I ever met."

They were quiet a minute. "You can't take him too seriously; he's just a hillbilly from Arkansas. It was the other NCO's who named him 'Mad Jack.' But he's a good sergeant. Knows what to look for in a soldier."

"What do you look for in a soldier?"

Brady sipped. "I guess I partly want a man who doesn't boss too easily. You ever see photographs of young Nazis saluting? They look so earnest, like they'd do whatever you say, like they turned their brains off. That's deadly. In battle, you have to be fully conscious.

"So many men just shut down. Some run. Some try to hide. Others just sacrifice themselves. As odd as it sounds, that's easier than taking responsibility for staying alive."

Brady rotated his beer glass to sip from the still-frosted part of the mug's rim. "I like a man that'll challenge me, up to a point. Not that he disobeys under fire -- I'll shoot a deserter as cheerfully as any captain in the Army -- but someone who's not comfortable doing something he doesn't understand, just because I say so.

"Weaker officers like yes-men, because they make you feel like a leader. But yes-men are less effective."

Brady leaned closer. "In battle, there's a very limited amount you can plan for. The men have got to figure it out and get after it, without waiting for you."

The waiter brought two more beers without asking.

Willem asked, "And what do you think of these men you're training right now?"

Brady laughed. "You talk about these men like you were hiring them for a job. Like they're your ticket back to Holland."

"You said that before, that first day in your office."

Brady's face showed surprise.

"You told me I was on probation, so you could make sure I got to know the men."

"Oh yeah. I remember now."

"Hightower's dad was a Cherokee who left when John was a baby. His mother works in a beauty parlor and they barely get by. John told me he spent two years in reform school because he took a tire tool to a bully in school who beat him up every day."

Brady curled his lower lip.

"Stringer was the foreman of a millroom in a tire plant before he got out of high school. He stood down a whole crowd of union men who were trying to shut down the plant.

"Green wants to be a writer, but knows he has no story."

Willem waited for Brady to say something. Instead Brady was looking at the waitress, as if he had already forgotten the topic, and was back in America after a good day's work.

"They all play baseball. Their team the Indians is playing in the camp championship game next week. It's Stringer's team, which is why they call it the Indians. But Ichinowski is the best player – fielder or batter. He plays shortstop, and at the plate he's a switch hitter."

Brady finally showed interest, with an inquisitive smile.

"Yes, I know what a switch hitter is."

Brady laughed. "OK."

Willem drained the last of his beer; his thirst from the exercises overpowered his distaste for the watery lager. He looked at Brady's glass goblet and saw it was empty too.

"Two's enough for me," Brady said. "Ready to go?"

"Sure. We don't want to run into any jezebels."

Brady laughed. "Where'd you get that?"

"Mad Jack warns us constantly."

Brady laughed again and shook his head. "Haggerty."

In the barracks, Axis Sally was on the air. Brady had said he did not want the men to listen to German radio; but he had not forbidden it.

What are your wives and girlfriends doing, Joe? They must be lonely. I'm a woman -- I can tell you.

Stringer and Ichinowski moved their lips provocatively and mocked her fake American slang. "Hey, Joe."

TOWARD HOME
May, 1944

Willem heard the two-and-a-half-ton trucks rumble to the barracks, and heard their plaintive brakes as they stopped in rows.

"Where we goin'?"

"South coast," Haggerty answered. "Means we're goin' soon."

On the truck's hard bed, the ride was uncomfortable and long. Lindell looked around. "Anybody scared?"

"Hell, we're all scared, I bet," Hall answered.

"What's the scaredest you've ever been?"

"What's it to you?" Glass answered.

"I'm just passin' the time."

After a silence, Lindell answered his own question. "Brother Joe rode bulls in the west Texas circuit. I was sittin' in the stands, wishin' somethin' interesting would happen like a bull catchin' a clown. Then Joe was on a bull and a horn went into his face. If you've ever seen bull-ridin,' you'd wonder why it doesn't happen more often. As soon as Joe hit the ground, there was already a pool of blood spreadin' away from his face. I jumped the fence and ran out where he was. The clowns had already cleared the bull. Joe was lyin' there, twitchin.' From the blood on the ground, I thought he couldn't have much left in him. What scared me most was the look on the clowns' faces: those are some hard birds to rattle, but you could tell they thought it was bad. I vomited right there.

"A clown drove us to the hospital. It turned out pretty minor; the horn went between his lips and cut the roof of his mouth. The hospital released Joe the next day with stitches. He was eatin' cold soup for a month, and then he was ridin' bulls again. But anyway, it sure scared me."

Glass said, "I was too ignorant to be afraid, but I was on ships out on Lake Superior that rolled past forty-five degrees during the November gales. I thought it was an adventure till I learned about other freighters capsizing in that kind of water. I can't remember ever being really afraid, but I should've been."

Ichinowski cleared his throat. "I was like you, too dumb to be afraid, but I was probably headed to jail. Mom and Dad worked away from the house, and I was on my own till dinner. Each day after school, my pal Doug and I ran wild all around Detroit. Doug was too much. We went to this dime ball game, semi-pro, and he actually gave an old man in the stands a hot foot, the way they do in comic books. Just a few days ago I got a letter saying Doug's in jail."

Hall said, "I'm afraid of stayin' on the farm and endin' up like Daddie, watchin' everyone else gettin' somewhere in life and feelin' jealous."

Lindell said, "Oh, I have a second scaredest-I've-ever-been story: I was in a storm shelter under a tornado."

Ichinowski said, "Nobody cares. You told your scary story already."

Gilker said, "When I was seventeen, I was on a joyride one night with some friends. The car spun off an eight-foot bank at forty or faster and rolled four times. I was in the passenger seat. The driver went through my window and needed two hundred stitches in his head and face. I came to in the back seat. I never had time to be afraid; I remember the sound of gravel and then waking up in the back. No pain until the next day."

"My worst fear came true," Douglass said. "When I played high school football, I was afraid I'd graduate without ever making a play and I did."

"What position?"

"End. I really was too small to play line and too slow to play anything else. Over and over, we ran this play in practice where the fullback and halfback came at me shoulder to shoulder to block for the other halfback. One hundred times out of a hundred, they put me on my back. I just wanted to do something: stand them up, break 'em up, anything but let them hit the linebackers like I hadn't even been there. It never happened. All day Coach screamed at everyone else: "'Boys, quit your grab-assin' around!'

"But Coach never accused me of 'grab-assin' around.' Whenever I got knocked down, he must have decided it was pure lack of ability."

"I'm afraid of dying anonymous," Green said.

"What do you mean?"

"Ten, twenty years after you die, it's as if you never lived."

They jostled on the flat wooden bed, until at last the trucks braked noisily and Mad Jack Haggerty opened the canvas doors in back. "Welcome to the Sausages. Your new home."

The drills became more specialized. They raced out of Higgins Boats in dry or wet weather, wind or calm, night or daylight. "God *damn* it," Haggerty shouted inches from their faces. "I wish I was a German and you girls was all I had to worry about!"

Haggerty timed their sprints from the Higgins Boat to the sand's landward edge. When they floundered Mad Jack shouted, "Oh, my Goodness! Fun for the Germans!"

Sometimes they debarked in water over their heads, sometimes waist-deep. They practiced getting in fast with heavy equipment.

"I'm turnin' you in for impersonatin' soldiers!"

Willem waited in line on the gangplank, sheltered by the troopship from the gathering wind.

Hall shifted his gear. "My God, it's slow gettin' this invasion off the ground."

Gilker chuckled. "Let's hope it's faster getting off this boat."

"Stop and start; stop and start. Two feet at a time, carryin' half our weight in gear."

"I'm throwin' half mine overboard: smokes, rubbers, VD pamphlets, French dictionaries. It'd be a miracle if I wound up needin' this stuff."

"Better hope no *Luftwaffe* planes come. We'd be easy targets."

"Not in this weather." Green looked nervously at the fast-moving clouds. "But I'd rather have clear skies for the crossing; we'll need air support when we beach."

Willem's gaze moved down the long snaking line of men waiting to board; for a moment he thought he knew the feeling of *Wehrmacht* soldiers waiting at the German border in 1940, exhilarated with mingled hope and terror.

At last the troopship left harbor in a thickening drizzle. Willem could not count all the vessels forming lines offshore.

"I wonder if the Germans can even imagine so many men, so many ships, coming to their beach."

"Jerry'd have to know," Stringer answered, "he's gonna get his ashes hauled."

Haggerty shouted, "Men! Listen up. Captain Brady's got something to say."

They turned to see Brady, his hand on the shoulder of a man wearing a beret and tricolor patch. "Men, we've got a last-minute addition: Etienne Brel, French commando. He'll interpret."

"We've already got an interpreter," Ichinowski protested. "Willem."

"This one's really French. Not my decision. Orders."

Willem stepped over to Brady and lowered his voice. "So it was a bluff, that first day in your office? I was attached to your company whether you approved or not? All that talk about making sure I fit in, you just made that up?"

Brady moved his hand across his mouth. "Yes, sir, I did. It's too late to say something like that to Etienne."

Willem laughed. "You know what? I don't care. It was good advice. Look at Etienne. He's alone on this landing. I'm not."

"You're right."

Wedged in the silent black hold, Willem suspected there were still others awake, but kept quiet anyway.

Boots clumped on the ship's ladder, and Brady's voice penetrated the dark. "Postponed. Weather's too bad. We'll stay out here and see if we can land day after tomorrow, June 6. Otherwise we'll unload and try in a few weeks."

A chorus of groans came.

"Jesus! This is bad on your nerves!"

For ten minutes no one spoke, until he heard Douglass' voice: "They say casualties the first twelve hours may be seventy percent."

Ichinowski's voice replied in the dark. "I'm not worried. Jerry's killed enough Polacks; statistically, I got to make it all the way to Berlin. But I do feel sorry for you guys."

Gilker said to Douglass, "James, sounds like you're getting nervous."

"No more than the next man."

"James, you thought about why you're taking all this risk?"

There was a pause in the dark. "My family always honored men who fought for freedom. Now I guess it's my turn."

Gilker snorted. "I bet you don't even know what freedom means."

"Everybody knows what it means!"

"If it's so simple, then tell me."

Lindell's voice came through the dark. "Gilker, give it a rest."

Douglass raised his voice. "If I have to tell you, there's something wrong with you."

"'This is the grave of James Douglass,'" Gilker spat with sarcasm. "'He died fighting for freedom. But he couldn't even say what it meant.'"

"You go to hell. I don't care what you say."

For a full minute no one spoke. Then Douglass's voice came through the dark.

"All right! Start with the 'four freedoms' Roosevelt talks about. What are they? 'Freedom from want, freedom from fear,...'"

A second snort came from Gilker. "Roosevelt'll call anything freedom, if it's something he wants to control. If Roosevelt decided your butt was too big, he'd put you in prison and call it 'Freedom from Douglass.' And when the Supreme Court called it unconstitutional, he'd just add new Justices, or threaten to, until the honest ones surrendered. You're risking your life so Roosevelt can do that?"

"Give up, James," Ichinowski said. "Gilker knows everything."

The rhythm of the Channel waves grew sensible against the hull.

Lindell sighed noisily. "How about you, Stephen? I bet you know why you're fighting. You must hate Nazis, the way they go after Jews."

The wave rhythm against the hull grew noticeable again.

Green said, "My grandparents came from Russia, where I think the persecution of Jews was pretty bad. They came through New Orleans to Omaha; my grandfather got work as a cutter in a meat plant. He was one of those really Jewish Jews, the kind that look like evil guys in stories. Looking back, he was fantastically kind to me. But when I was a kid, he looked so exotic, so strange."

For an instant Green slowed, as if he expected to be interrupted. Then he said, "My dad was very different from Grandpa. He didn't encourage us to learn Russian or Yiddish; in fact he did the least religious observance he could do without showing disrespect. We kids always ate fried chicken and beef stew; played country club sports like golf and tennis. He never said it in so many words, but at some point, I realized he didn't want me to seem like a Jew. Looking back, I think the message was: 'Don't be like us. Fit in.'"

Green paused again. "So Hitler doesn't have to get rid of Judaism. Where I grew up, the Jews are getting rid of it."

"Maybe," Ichinowski said, "he just likes golf and tennis."

Lindell interrupted. "Well, I have a favor to ask you all. If I wind up dying for freedom or the Hebrew religion or the liberation of Dutchmen, I hope some of you will check on my family. Ruth'll have enough money to live on, and my brother will help out. But I'm scared of my children growing up without a father. I hope somebody'll take my son fishing. I hope some man I can trust'll spend time with my daughter and make her feel special."

Hall's voice came through the dark. "Where is it exactly you live?"

"San Angelo. West Texas, in case you didn't know."

"Sounds hard to get to."

They heard Lindell spit. "Well I guess I won't count on you."

"I'll get there, you irritable son of a bitch. I just wanted you to realize it's a lot of trouble."

"Maybe I'm worried for nothing. Surely I can't be killed, because not a single one of you birds could be trusted to bring the music of Jimmy Rodgers to France."

Willem's accent marked his voice in the dark. "Let me tell you all something. You know the most important thing in determining whether a wounded man will live, assuming he's not shot in the brain or the heart?"

"What's that?"

"*Believing* he'll live."

There was silence again.

"I'll make a deal with every one of you: if you get wounded on the beach, and you're still alive by the time I reach you, I'll keep you alive. I guarantee it. All you have to do is stay alive till I reach you."

"All right," several voices chorused.

Lindell sang. Willem was sure he heard it wrong.

Ole Miss Queen was feelin' mean
Till she caught her hand in the washin' machine.
She's movin' on.

Brady nudged Willem. "Hey."

"Yes?"

"I think everyone's asleep."

"Maybe."

Brady lit a small flashlight and handed Willem an unsealed envelope.

"What is it?"

"A letter to my son. Finally put it down on paper, just in case. I want you to keep it, and mail it if anything happens to me."

Willem felt his pockets for a safe place.

Brady nudged him. "Read it first."

"What do you mean?"

"You're going to be in salt water. You may get shot yourself and bleed on it, God knows what. So you may have to rewrite it. I want to know you can read my handwriting, or even remember it, if you have to."

Willem pulled out the paper, unfolded it and read, with Brady holding the flashlight.

Dear Kevin,

You may not remember, but when you were little, whenever you had just done something, you'd look up and ask, "Daddy, are you proud of me?" I always said yes and I meant it. I was proud of you and I still am.

But to be a man, you'll have to ask, "Am I proud of me?" It'll be your answer that counts. Let others give you advice and information, but only that. Save for yourself the question of who's proud of you.

I wish I knew some way to say this more clearly. I'm afraid you'll read this and not understand. So I hope I get a chance to tell you in person. But if you get this letter, that means I couldn't. If that happens, I'm asking you to make it your mission to understand this and make it part of your life. It's the main thing I would have wanted to tell my only son.

Love,
Dad

Something tightened inside Willem, as if his windpipe were trying to escape through his mouth. Suddenly he knew Brady, grasped the impulse choking its way painfully out through words, like a long childbirth.

"I understand," he told Brady. "And if I live, I'll find Kevin and tell him. I won't finish till I know he understands."

Willem wondered what someone would tell Geertruide and Herbert for him, if he died tomorrow.

A RECKONING
June 6, 1944

By 5:50 the shock and noise were unimaginable. Through the observation hole, Werner Kessler had a clear view of the landing craft moving south, and the great battleships farther out, so many that it seemed the sea had sprouted with gray vessels all the way to the horizon. He knew the bombardment would lift for the landing, and that when it did, he would have to scramble to re-check the gun sightings. Till then, there was nothing to do but absorb a concussion so extreme that after each blast he found himself surprised to be alive and conscious.

As the minutes passed, the landing craft never approached his shore, but pushed southward past him. Maybe they would not land here after all.

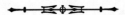

The troopship rolled in four-foot surf. Willem's squad bobbed with the ship's roll as they spidered down the netting into the Higgins Boat.

"Seven miles from France," Brady announced. "Should hit the beach at 6:30."

From the distant shore, German artillery began to pound, but the battleship gunnery answered, louder and more continuous than before, as if the dueling artillery were lions contending for mastery over the pride, each determined by the depth of its utterance to prove itself the fiercer, the surer of its claim. Willem stuffed his allotted two fluffs of cotton into his ears.

In the middle of the Higgins Boat, Green shouted through the noise and the ear cottons. "Listen to that. I bet you could hear this on the moon."

Kelsey, the English coxswain, steered the Higgins Boat toward the beach that no one could see. Brady stood near Kelsey in back, Haggerty with the front row at the bow ramp. Through the wind and the shelling, Willem heard Haggerty shout to Carbone and Glass, "Alright, boys. If anybody was ever trained to take a beach, it's you. No kidding, right now you may actually be the most dangerous soldiers the world has ever seen."

At 6:15, bombers flying beachward filled the sky, filling Willem's entire view. It occurred to him there was no limit to what the Americans and the British were bringing to fight the Germans, and it seemed that fear was the only thing that could stop them. Willem scanned his companions' silent faces.

Stringer regretted eating no breakfast. Now he had nothing to vomit, and shook instead with a nausea of dry air. He looked at

Haggerty's swollen cheek and thought of the tobacco juice inside, then began to sweat in the cool air.

Green thought of summer construction jobs, where he had heard the fighting words of Omaha's roughest men: "I'll clean your clock . . . I'll knock your dick in the dirt." It had scared and even impressed him in those days. Now it seemed stupid bravado, with no meaning against the killing proficiency ahead. Green hoped he would maintain the composure to follow all that he had learned. As the Higgins boat lurched, Green leaned back, waiting for the moment his training would prove out, one way or the other.

Douglass thought of his mother, a "difficult" woman who had always done what she thought was right. He could not imagine his mother in the Higgins Boat. But he certainly could not imagine her running away.

Ichinowski felt the hot, bittersweet sting of vomit lap against his sinuses. He stared at the inside wall of the craft.

Glass had an advantage over them all. Crewing on the big freighters that worked Lake Superior in all weather, he had stood on decks tilted at crazy angles, and today he needed no handhold. The feel of the boat floor against his soles, rolling from heel to ball in reaction to the surf, spurred his adrenaline. Glass was the only enlisted man who spoke, encouraging his friends, who looked sick and white-faced.

Lindell conjured the tough old rodeo men he had met at his brother's competitions. Surely they would not be afraid; he tried to feel what he imagined they would feel.

Hall tried to stand upright as the landing craft churned in the unwelcoming sea. He tried to recall the fiery banjo music that he and his father both loved, hillbilly tunes he had called to mind on marches and maneuvers, imagining this morning and stirring his courage. But against the surf and the unforgiving shellfire, the banjo music seemed silly. He felt his lower intestine sag, his face warmed, and his lower lip quivered. He wondered if he could maintain his composure.

Brady moved slowly among the packed men, gripping the boat gunnels or a man's shoulders to maintain his balance. Brady gave no sign that he saw Hall's swelling panic, but just leaned into Hall's face and spoke a little toughly. "Listen, Hall. I can't have any heroical bullshit out of you. We're gonna need you on the way to Paris, so keep your head down, get to shelter as fast as you can, try to see who's shooting at you, and then find the safest way to get a grenade on 'em. No heroical bullshit. We clear?"

Brady moved on without a response. Hall breathed deeply, newly steady, and his fear no longer felt shameful. He knew he could channel his fear and follow Brady's instructions.

Hightower thought of his mother, of her white, thinnish face and silvering hair, the mirth that had not yet gone completely out of her eyes, his only totem of anything holy. Then his mother drifted from his mind. The sides rose too high to see the beach, so he simply rocked with the boat, the old familiar anger rising, an anger that felt today like a sure friend.

Every man knew the coxswains' orders: unload the men at wading depth, and return for the next squad without risking the craft.

As coxswain, Kelsey was the first on Boat 32 with a view of the beach. From the German bunkers, machine-gun fire found its range and churned the water audibly, ringing against the steel hull. As other boats began to lower ramps, the men on Boat 32 heard the screams of a massacre. Hearing it, all the men watched Kelsey's tight, unconfident face.

"This far out," Kelsey shouted, "You haven't got a chance. I see a reach where the water's deeper close to shore. I can get you almost to the high-water mark."

Machine gun fire laced the hull as Kelsey angled right. A bullhorn from the command craft, LCI 15, echoed through the noise: "Boat 32, unload where you are and return. Boat 32, unload and return. Boat 32, unload and return."

The men watched for Kelsey's reaction. His face purpled and his mouth barely moved as he muttered. Only those nearest could hear: "Boat 15, blow it out yer ass."

Kelsey held his angle and speed. The men watched his face, knowing he had exposed himself for their protection. At last his Boat 32 grounded and the ramp chains whirred as they slung. Kelsey shouted, "It's as close as I can get!" The hoarse goodbye muffled into the noise as men clambered forward.

Sergeant Mad Jack Haggerty shouted, "This is it! Let's heat 'em up!"

As the ramp angled down, Willem first saw it. He saw it beyond the bobbing heads, beyond the shoulders and upturned weapons of his friends, and beyond the churning sea-foam: Normandy's brown-gray sand.

In the water, Hall lost his footing as tracer bullets splashed around him; it seemed impossible that none had touched him. Then the headless trunk of an engineer drifted near. Hall pushed the corpse forward like a shield, crouching as he waded behind it, feeling the body absorb the soft pounding of bullets. As the shallow water met the sand, Hall was still nearly prone, unwilling to lose the shielding corpse. Then he saw little wakes as bullets exited the engineer's skin; the protection of the engineer's flesh had been an illusion. Hall pushed the body aside and rushed for the sheltering rise unshielded, crouching as he moved, so hopeless of living he did not even run full speed. At the little rise, amazed to find himself alive, he dropped and breathed hard with his face against the cool sand.

He pulled his weapon to him, checked its clip, then aimed it toward the German lines, raising his head slightly and looking for a target.

Lindell relived the moment, years before, when he had raced a tornado's fronting gusts to the family storm cellar. The tornado had turned every object into a missile, swirling and shooting past the soft bodies running to shelter. The ground had shaken with such urgency it seemed to say, "Do not rely on me; I am no longer the familiar earth." Lindell had kept his head down and run to his father's shouted commands until they closed the cellar door behind him. Now Lindell ducked his head again and sprinted to the base of the bluffs.

Douglass spilled into the churn and moved to a burning tank, twenty yards inshore from the foaming water. The steel skin of the burning tank scorched his hand, but he could not move back without entering the path of German cross-fire.

"Oh, Lord."

Douglass looked backward at the mass of damaged vehicles, at corpses bobbing in the water, at wounded men sitting at water's edge, too stunned to fear the bullets spraying sand around them, just what Brady had warned against: a mob in place of an army.

Douglass saw Kelsey's Boat 32, reversed at full throttle, but unable to clear the hull in the shallow water. It was only a matter of time before Boat 32 would be hit.

As far as Douglass could tell, he was the only man unwounded on his part of the beach, but he felt compelled to help Kelsey. He moved again to the tank's edge and saw the gunnery source midway up the gentlest slope and to his right.

Behind, and out past the beach, three destroyers surged into view. Two flew the Stars and Stripes; the third flag was a mystery. The destroyers overmatched the German guns and moved closer, their crews less vulnerable than the infantry to machine-gun fire, unwilling for the battle to be lost. Douglass watched the three destroyers, coming to help like a big brother on the playground.

Now Douglass' mind began to resolve itself, and the chemicals in men's brains that change fear to decision began to work in him. Peering again past the tank edge, he timed the intervals between the gun bursts, then lifted the heavy Browning Automatic Rifle, waited for the machine-gun sweep to pass, pulled the trigger and held it. The heavy B.A.R. recoiled chunkily against his shoulder, and he saw its discharge bite pieces of concrete from around the bunker eye.

Douglass paused. The casemate guns were still firing; he was pretty sure he had not killed any Germans. But the German gunner changed his pattern, apparently having noticed Douglass. Maybe he was taking some pressure off the men coming ashore. At last, he told himself, at last he was contributing to the goddamned fight.

On the beach, Gilker heard the beginning of an explosion and then silence. Something heavy had punched his abdomen and thrown him on the ground where he looked skyward, unable to move. A shooting pain roamed his upper back. But more alarming was the dizzy weakness, the encompassing cold and nausea.

A private knelt and looked at his abdomen. "Jesus Christ." Eyes showing disgust and fear, the private moved away without giving aid.

Gilker was sure he was dying. He leaned his head further back and breathed more deeply. If he just concentrated on not dying, if he could let everything else go, not fear the explosions, not care who won or lost the battle, just concentrate on not dying, maybe he could overcome the feeling that life was flowing out of him. He focused on not dying and began to convince himself he was incredibly strong.

The Dutch doctor, Willem, was there. Hoarding his tiny strength, Gilker begrudged even talking, but Willem seemed to know what he was thinking. "Look at you. My God, you're a strong one," Gilker heard him say. Willem sprinkled sulfa; Gilker could neither see nor feel precisely where.

Willem gripped Gilker's hand. "I can give you morphine if the pain's too bad, but I'd rather keep you conscious so you can help me diagnose. Ryan, squeeze my hand if you have to have morphine."

Gilker understood he had a chance, and kept his hand still.

"Now, squeeze my hand with two squeezes if you understand and you don't need morphine."

Gilker squeezed twice.

"Good. Very good. I wish every patient were as strong as you; I'd never lose one."

A medic appeared. Gilker heard Willem say, "This looks worse than it is. The skin's torn up and swelling fast, but the vitals are OK. I know this man; he's the strongest in the platoon. Keep him off morphine if he can tolerate the pain. Get him to that ledge and keep him still. Find out how soon you can get him onto a boat."

He turned to Gilker. "I'll be back. But you're OK."

At the burning tank, Hightower and Stringer, red-faced and breathing hard, had joined Douglass.

"Where did you come from?"

"Looking for you," Stringer answered.

Hightower seemed unaware that his left ear was gone, with a blood-red ring in its place.

Now Willem reached them too. On Willem's forearms the soaking blood was half-dried, darkening to blackberry pulp.

Hightower shifted to face Willem. "You're wearing a few gallons of blood there."

"So far, none of it's mine."

Douglass pointed at the casement he had fired on. "That's a tough approach. Two hundred yards?"

"Give me grenades," Willem said. Willem stuffed grenades around his bandolier and left the tank's shelter toward the German nest, bent at the waist.

From behind he heard Hightower grunt "Let's go!" He glimpsed them following, Hightower and Stringer with their rifles, Douglass with the heavy Browning Automatic just behind.

Before them the casemate exploded from the direct hit of a destroyer's shell. They dropped in momentary shock, until they saw the casemate crumble and go silent. They rose again and charged with weapons at level.

Hightower and Willem leapt into the nest to find a few wounded survivors. Douglass and Stringer followed seconds later. Willem felt a moment's exultation just to stand in a German nest, safe for a moment, with so many defenders dead and prisoners around him.

"Look." Douglass pointed back at Kelsey's boat; the waters around it were quiet.

Sergeant Haggerty crawled fast along the sand's crest, his crawling arms looking like a dwarf's bow legs. As if unsure of Lindell's sprinted path through the barbed wire and mines, Haggerty collected grenades from wounded and dead men and threw them kneeling, in a sequence that cleared a path to the bluff, then leapt up and ran like a lunatic to show the way.

Now Captain Brady strutted parallel to the water's edge, tall and exposed as if the gunfire were only sleet, firing a pistol at the bunkers, replacing clips from a stack in his hand.

"Let's get on with it! There's nothing to do on this beach but get killed. Let's move up and stay alive!"

Seeing Haggerty's and Brady's example, the unwounded men behind the stranded boats, or scattered on the beach, ran low to the dunes, ditched for a moment, then rose and followed Haggerty's trail.

At the bluff, some crawled up, taking safety in the little hollows and gullies. Some threw ropes and hooks to the top.

Hall, Green and Stringer reached the top first, parallel and ten yards apart, found the first defensive trench empty, and gained speed with an adrenaline rush as they trotted around it.

The second trench was fully manned. The attackers and defenders saw each other at the same time; with no cover the Americans reflexively dropped to a knee and fired. Their first shots missed, and the Germans' answering rounds missed them, too. It seemed for an instant that the guns were misfiring, but the shell cases in the air and on the ground proved the rapid firing real. Suddenly Hall rose again, as if he could not tolerate waiting for a shooter to find him as he continued to miss, and sprinted toward point blank.

Green and Stringer seemed to waver, as if to follow Hall ran against every intuition, but to let him die alone was unimaginable. Before they could act, the trench ahead exploded, as Haggerty, Ichinowski, Lindell and Glass were visible moving through them.

One more trench lay ahead. German boys sprang up in surrender, raising their arms as if to shield their faces, one of them sobbing like the child that he was. Hall and Green fired into the boys, in the way that a farmer kills a harmless snake before his first reaction of fear can cool.

Willem sat with Brady and Green, looking downhill at the company, immobile from exhaustion. Brady said, "God. What these boys did today: any honest man who saw, would wonder if he could have stood it."

Willem did not know what to say.

Brady went on: "Where's their Homer? Who's going to tell their story?"

It was only now that Willem noticed Brady's foot wound. Wordlessly he unwrapped Brady's boot and sock. "You'll have to go to the hospital ship."

Brady pulled phlegm through his nose and tried to laugh. "This will make HQ suspicious. It's the kind of wound men give themselves, when they're afraid to fight." He snorted again. "I just got the sequence wrong."

Willem said, "If you didn't want any heroes, you set a bad example. You were walking on the beach like a movie cowboy."

"By the time I stood up, the danger was a lot less. Did you see what those destroyers did to the casemates?" Brady laughed at last, the way a child laughs who has been crying until a moment before. "But I was still scared to death, just trying not to show it. Part of the captaining business is good acting."

Brady looked around, as if unused to being the subject of conversation. Then he whispered, "If I'd done a perfect job training those men, what I did on the beach would have been unnecessary."

They grew silent and listened to the others, who faced the Channel as they spoke.

"Well, if that wasn't a genuine ten-pound baby girl of a landing, I don't know what would be," they could hear Haggerty say.

"How long were we on the beach?"

"I'm not sure."

Everyone stared at the vessels below, still unloading men and equipment. On the sand, burial details arranged corpses on white mattress covers; riflemen checked their gear and moved inland; engineers marked logistics zones.

"Look at those people."

Willem understood. The beachcomber's energy and activity seemed incomprehensible.

"We were lucky."

"I bet every other squad lost more than we did."

"It was Kelsey."

"That was his name? The coxswain?"

"Kelsey."

"'Boat 15, blow it out yer ass.'"

"That son of a bitch."

"He finally got off the sand bar?"

"I think so. I quit looking back."

"I think so."

"That son of a bitch."

"How's Gilker?"

Haggerty answered before Willem. "None too extra."

"He'll live," Willem said. "He'll live."

"Where's Carbone?"

"Dead," Willem answered. "Head wound in the water. Died instantly."

Willem had seen Anthony Carbone fall face-down in the surf, and seen the messy exit wound in the back of his head. Bending on his own sturdy legs, Willem had carried him to a low dune, then removed Carbone's thin necklace and cross to give to Brady.

Lieutenant Gerber, the Company Executive Officer, had stayed too long at the sand crest, until a mortar concussion lifted him then dropped him again, body unmarred, his teeth biting into the peaceful sand. Willem had held a mirror to Gerber's mouth, found no condensation, and known the lieutenant was dead.

"I knew Carbone the least."

"He never talked about his family."

"I'm not sure I ever saw him laugh."

The conversation stopped.

"They say a dying man's last thoughts are about his mother."

For a moment Willem imagined Carbone's mother, how she showed her love, how she held him and spoke to him, what kind of treats she gave him. Then he cut off his own silly thoughts. That's not why a dying man thinks of his mother, he thought. The image of his mother is only the reflection of his own soul.

His mind went to Sophia.

"Good Lord," Lindell said. "I almost forgot." He sang hoarsely:

Now, the hold-up men all know me
And they sure leave me be.
I'm a pistol-packin' papa,
And I ramble where I please.

You can take my new sport roadster.
You can take my hard-boiled hat.
But you can never take from me
My silver-mounted Gatt.

When you hear my pistol poppin'
You'd better hide yoself some place.
'Cause I ain't made for stoppin,'
And I come from a shooting race.

I'm a pistol-packin' papa
And I'm going to have my fun.
Just follow me and you will hear
The barking of my gun.

Hall tried to spit. "It's supposed to be a cheerful song," he said. "I was tryin," Lindell answered.

In the chapel, Sophia wondered if she heard the broadcast correctly. "*El tio es frances ahora.*"

Willem was at Normandy. According to Radio *Oranje*, the landings had succeeded. How many weeks to Rhenen?

FRENCH SUMMER
June, 1944

Erwin stared at the braised pork on the lump of sauerkraut on his plate. The enemy were still in France. No word from Kessler and Zimmer.

Why had the *Wehrmacht* never summoned him? Even children and old men were called now to fight, but not Erwin. Often now his mind wandered to imaginary confrontations in Berlin, speaking to senior staff he had never actually met, defending charges against his conduct that no one had ever made.

His mind absently conjured Vogel and Strohn, dying at Kursk. His thoughts drifted then to his own lost son.

"Colonel Schell," Geertruide's voice broke through. "You're not listening."

Erwin looked up. "What's that?"

"I asked what German families do for Christmas."

Christmas? He forced a smile. "Well, we have an evergreen tree we call '*Tannenbaum.*' We sing around it, and then we share a wonderful dinner."

Geertruide seemed satisfied with the answer, and he stared again at the pork. Were Kessler and Zimmer alive at Normandy?

When he saw the clock, Erwin jumped. Had he ever slept till eight fifteen before? The curtains were closed, so the room was still nearly dark. But in the dimness, resting on the covers over his legs, he saw a white rectangle. He reached for the envelope, left the bed and pulled the curtains to admit the daylight. The envelope bore the same archaic German calligraphy as the warning he had gotten, his first week in Holland.

He slipped his finger through the seal and pulled out a long letter. The script he instantly recognized.

> *I knew you'd worry, and persuaded my handler to allow a letter. He insists one letter only.*
>
> *We all agree I cannot return safe from the SS. My only hope for freedom is a German withdrawal. My handler has moved me to a remote place, where a group of old sisters have offered their attic.*
>
> *In this place, Germans are rare. But in case any NSB ever check the house, I'm a tuberculosis patient with a forged identity card. No one knows what neighbor to trust, and the sisters will be shot if they're caught, so I stay inside always. No exceptions! I take what food the women can offer, drink tea with them before bed, and read. So much sitting! It's hard to describe: away from everyone I know, with a new onderduiker name. I have become just a man in a shirt in a room.*

One night, on the sisters' bookshelf, I found a German title called Nationaloekonomie, by Ludwig von Mises. It belonged to their nephew, a student who died at Grebbeberg. I can't tell you how the sight of German in print cheered me up. I carried the book upstairs and started to read its thousand pages. Evidently this Von Mises was an Austrian, a university professor. He published his book in Switzerland just before the western invasion. Can you imagine a German publishing an economics book in 1940? Like a moon, floating free from earth's gravity.

At some point I realized the book was a defense of capitalism. I wouldn't have finished if I'd had anything else to do. But upstairs alone so much, I kept reading. Somewhere I thought of General Langer's joke. Do you remember? He said, "It takes a German to fight a German." Maybe it takes a German to persuade one, too. I feel strange telling you this, but it's impossible to understand Von Mises and accept National Socialism – or any other socialism. I felt disloyal to you, but strangely exhilarated. I wish we could talk about it.

From my handler's war news, I foresee the time we can meet again; I look forward to it more than I can say. I am certain this is my only letter, so until peacetime I am

Your son,
Reinhard

Alive, then.

In odd circumstances, but alive. Erwin felt a warm surge from his chest to his face, and for a moment he thought he might weep.

Nationaloekonomie. Ludwig von Mises. An Austrian? Surely no copy here at Paardenveld, and surely none in the Third Reich. Guse was an excellent student. But who knows what delusions he might have fallen victim to, isolated in some attic?

"Thank you for delivering last night's letter," Erwin told Sophia.

She looked bewildered so he handed her Guse's letter, with the calligraphied envelope. At the sight of the lettering, she looked at him again. Erwin just returned her gaze, until she opened the letter and read.

"Thank God," she breathed. "An *onderduiker*."

"What's that?"

"Someone who 'dived under.' Hiding from the Germans."

"How do you know such things?"

She looked into his eyes without turning away or looking down, until he forgot his question, and together they savored the news.

"Can you tell me . . .?" When he saw Sophia's unresponsive gaze, Erwin didn't finish the question.

Sophia said, "He seems to think the war will end soon."

They were quiet again until Erwin spoke. "It's the Farm Inspector, isn't it?"

Sophia seemed to flinch before she recovered and answered him coolly, "Whoever it is, he saved your son's life."

Erwin reached to take the letter back. "I should destroy this."

"Help me," Brady said from his stretcher on the beach. "What is it?" Willem asked.

"I want to finish this letter to Carbone's parents while it's on my mind."

Brady tore up a filled page and threw the wad onto a stack of other wads. "I've started over five or ten times. I wanted to say their son died, not only bravely, but as an indispensable member of the forces of justice in the most important battle in the most important war in the history of the world. I actually believe that.

But it comes out like propaganda, like I thought their son's death was acceptable."

"Can you think better if I write for you? You just tell me what you want to say?"

"I think so," Brady answered. "And maybe better too if I just quit trying to say anything profound. Try this."

Brady spoke slowly, giving himself time to think and Willem time to write:

Dear Mr. and Mrs. Carbone,

> *It is my sad duty to tell you your beloved son Anthony died this morning from a machine gun bullet. He died instantly and without pain.*
> *Anthony's unit was the first to confront the German defenses on his assigned beach. I have never seen an engagement that required more courage. Anthony never hesitated. In all the time I knew Anthony, I never heard him express fear or reluctance.*
> *I realize that knowing of your son's incredible heroism cannot lessen your grief.*

Respectfully,

Edward Brady
Captain, United States Army

Willem enclosed the cross and necklace which Brady now handed back to him.

Werner Kessler, the Koblenz boy who grew up in love with the sea, inhaled and exhaled slowly in the near-dark. As far as he could tell, the westernmost Americans had landed about one kilometer south. Three days of continuing gunfire meant the enemy was still ashore. Unless Rommel threw them back into the sea, it was only a matter of time until they reached his bunker.

Surely it was time for Kessler to return to a tank squadron, for the counter-attack. "*Nein*," they had said, Normandy was not the main enemy landing. Until the real thrust was clear, all tanks would be kept ready, away from the coast. Meanwhile, stay in your coastal bunker and steady your troops, they told him.

The tepid drinking water had gone foul, then run out. By day Kessler wore only his pants, boots and a thin undershirt. Each night, for warmth, he dressed again in his filthy uniform.

One of his Rumanians had become hysterical. Kessler had opened the door and let him leave, for certain death. The sullen *Osttruppen* still in the bunker spoke little. Kessler's sword and scabbard, leaning in shadow against the inner wall, now seemed silly and useless.

It would all be endurable if only Colonel Schell were here, or even one of the Myrmidons, from whose company he had drawn so much resolution. Zimmer the brewer, Strohn the philosopher, Vogel with his fierce eyes, or Guse the giant.

As he looked at his sword, grenades flew into the observation hole and their concussion dizzied him to the bunker floor. So near the life-giving sea, Kessler died with only a moment's first glimpse of the flame-thrower curling through the bunker window.

John Stringer pointed at the barges unloading tires on the artificial dock offshore. "Smell that rubber. You can smell it from here. It stays in your nostrils, huh?"

"I smell it."

"All the way from Akron."

"Big deal." Ron Ichinowski's lips spread in a smile. "Look at all those jeeps and deuce-and-a-half's. All the way from Detroit."

To Willem, Omaha Beach smelled mainly of dead livestock, and corpses still waiting for burial.

"Jesus," Forrest Hall said. "Bring some lime. This is worse than the landing."

"We're running out of space to unload, unless we push the perimeter farther in," Robert Glass said.

"Look," Hightower pointed inland. Long lines of paratroopers in special tunics swaggered through the perimeter.

Glass studied their faces. "That must have been tough duty."

Stringer answered, "Landing behind enemy lines at night, having to find your squad . . ."

With a cheerful, matter-of-fact tone, Sergeant Haggerty asked, "Know what scares jumpers the most?"

Everyone looked at Haggerty blankly.

"Think about it. All the shots are coming from below. Imagine gittin' your manhood shot off."

Ichinowski said, "I've heard that, too. In the plane they sit on their helmets."

"Could a helmet stop flak?"

"Probably not, but it's an emotional thing."

Buster Lindell laughed. "You don't have to be a paratrooper to lose your fries. At home there was an old Spanish American War veteran, with a horrible limp. No one knew exactly how he'd been wounded. One day in town a girl asked him. He just looked at her and said, 'Young lady, if it was you, they'd have missed you completely.'"

Hall chuckled. "Brother McKelvey at our church had been an Army Chaplain at the Argonne. One time he started talkin' about the time he got 'shot in the Testament.' Finally pulled a Bible out of his coat and showed me where it stopped a bullet. I said, 'I thought you meant something else.'"

A hedgerow, three meters high, lined the sunken farm lane.

"That's as stout as a wall," Haggerty said.

"It's a thousand years old," Willem answered.

Only a gap led into the field behind. They had their instructions. Stringer put a fresh magazine in his Browning automatic rifle and checked its action. He pulled a deep breath, exhaled, then ducked into the gap. Haggerty nodded to Green, who followed.

They could hear Stringer's B.A.R. erupting, then felt the return fire of the German machine gun rattling the hedgerow. A mortar explosion lifted Stringer's heavy body in a rag-doll heap, visible over the hedge-top, before it dropped back to the ground. Stringer's B.A.R. was silent, and they heard Green cry out, "I'm hit!"

Glass moved through the gap but fell heavily back, with three bullet entries smoking in his chest. Willem pulled Glass away from the opening, but the eyes were already unblinking.

From the other side they could still hear Green warble, "I'm hit. God, I'm hit."

Haggerty stuck a helmet on a rifle muzzle, and poked it into the gap. A German bullet rang the helmet like a bell, and whipped the rifle out of his grip.

Willem unrolled his red-cross armband and thrust the crude banner into the gap, twitching with fear that his hands would be shot off. When he was sure the red cross was visible and heard no machine gun fire, Willem stepped in the gap, holding the armband over his head, afraid even to look up at the gunfire's source, shuddering with the conviction another burst would come.

On the ground, Green twisted painfully by Stringer's corpse. Stringer's lifeless eyes bulged with a final expression of surprise. Willem leaned over Green and found two bloody holes in his hip. Willem turned to make sure the enemy could see the red cross on his helmet. Still shaking with the expectation of a bullet, Willem lifted Green.   Green's voice burst out loudly as the lifting pressured his wounds. Breathing hard with fear, Willem carried Green through the gap and onto the sunken lane, out of the path of any gunfire.

"Your hip's shattered." Willem stuffed gauze into the wounds and looked up. "He's going to need blood, now."

Lindell and Hightower unfolded a stretcher, eased Green painfully on, and carried him down the lane.

Haggerty frowned. "How'd it look in there?"

"It's a square," Willem answered. "Made of hedgerows just like this one. There's another gap on the opposite corner."

"They must have had mortars pre-sighted on the gap, machine guns too." Haggerty stroked his own face. "Anyway. I think that's enough for one day."

"Look." James Douglass pointed a hundred yards away. "There are plenty of other holes. Maybe they're not all defended."

Haggerty spat. "Hard to believe they wouldn't be."

They sat in silence. Finally, Haggerty spat again. "Well every unit in Normandy shouldn't all get killed figuring out the same problem. Hall, walk east down the road and see what everybody else is doin' about this. Ichinowski, you go west. Don't be gone too long."

Hall knelt when he returned. "I found a whole platoon wiped out, with only the lieutenant to tell the story."

Ichinowski shook his head. "Up and down the line. Worse than the beach."

"Intelligence had to know about this terrain," Douglass complained. "Surely we planned for it."

"Who's 'we'?" Haggerty asked.

Ichinowski said, "Why not just roll a tank over the top? I'd go in, with a tank in front of me."

"All right," Haggerty answered. He looked toward the beach road. "Ichinowski, walk back down to Battalion. Tell 'em our captain's on a hospital boat and we'll take a tank for a replacement."

Forty-five minutes later, Ichinowski came up the beach road, alongside Lindell and Hightower in the narrow noon shadow.

"A tank's coming," Ichinowski said.

"Did they say when?"

"I asked but they wouldn't say."

"Oh well." Haggerty looked around. "Let's eat."

"How's Green?" Willem asked Lindell and Hightower.

"Full of morphine. Happy as a goddamned lark."

At two o'clock a handful of tanks rolled up the beach road, each turning right or left onto the farm lane.

"I guess we weren't the only ones with the tank idea."

Two tanks passed at full speed, before a third slowed and stopped at their gap. A sergeant spoke from the hatch. "You need us to cross the hedgerow?"

Haggerty strode toward him. "Yeah. Want us to make a little runway?"

The sergeant scanned the hedge. "I don't think so. Other side's the same slope?"

Willem stepped toward the tank. "Pretty much, yes."

"Then we'll be all right."

Haggerty looked up at the sergeant. "We'll get some men behind you, as soon as you're clear. We'll scout for you and cover."

"Especially if you see a *Panzerfaust* aimed at us," the sergeant answered.

"OK."

"OK."

The tank made a wide approach, then climbed the hedgerow. The tank's front edged above the top, like a turtle clambering out of a pond, pointing skyward and its underside exposed. An explosion shook and lit the tank, and a second explosion followed quickly inside. Momentum still carried the tank forward till it fell, disabled, on the other side. Willem could hear the muffled screams of the tank crew crescendo and stop inside.

Now they heard tanks up and down the lane exploding.

Haggerty spat. "Just what we should've have avoided: everbody learning the same lesson at once."

July, 1944

Nagel tapped the open door. "Excuse me, but you have a visitor. An SS major."

Erwin looked up. "Show him in."

An earnest young man with dark hair stopped at the appropriate distance and saluted. "Major Manfred Pelz, replacing Colonel Schmidt as the local SS superintendent."

Erwin returned the salute.

The young major began spoke with every sign of respect. "A great honor, Colonel Schell. I've read your file, and know your accomplishments."

Major Pelz's sheer seriousness drew Erwin to him. He could imagine that, years ago, he had made the same impression Pelz now made.

Erwin gestured to the chairs. "Sit down, *Bitte*. Coffee? Cigarette?"

"*Nein, danke.*"

"Cognac?"

"No, you're very kind."

There was a silence.

"Colonel Schell, I have some interest in Colonel Schmidt's murder."

"I can imagine. Shall I tell you what I know?"

"*Bitte.*"

"We arrested a Netherlander named Hogeboom in his house, with bloody clothes. Some of his possessions were in the murder room."

"You executed this Hogeboom, I believe."

"We did, and I referred ten reprisals, taken from the list in the NSB office."

"Normal procedure would be to deliver this Hogeboom to the SS for interrogation."

Erwin nodded. "I acted in haste. I acknowledged this to my own superior, General Langer."

"There's a suspicion that this Hogeboom would have difficulty accomplishing his crime alone."

"I understand. And you're about to say that finding Hogeboom's accomplices will be much harder with him dead."

Major Pelz nodded, with no expression of rebuke. There was another long silence.

"Colonel Schell, do you still have the reprisal list?"

"Possibly."

"If you can find it, and send it to me in town, it may figure into the investigation."

"Fine."

Silence again.

"You share this house with a Netherlandish woman, I believe."

"When I first came, and made it my headquarters, I let her and the children stay. In a separate wing."

"I understand Colonel Schmidt may have caused this woman some . . . . concern . . . ."

"You would have been ashamed, I hope. They did not behave like soldiers." Erwin had slurred Schmidt so plainly; he watched to see if Pelz had taken offense. Instead Major Pelz nodded, as calmly as if Erwin had said it was raining.

"And I believe your lieutenant, a Reinhard Guse, intervened."

"He did."

"Lieutenant Guse is your adopted son?"

"He is."

"You arrested the lieutenant?"

"Yes."

"May I ask, Sir, what arrangement you made for his captivity?"

"I locked him in the dairy shed."

"Without guard?" Even now, Major Pelz's tone was unruffled. They could have been discussing horses.

"Without guard."

"Do you know what became of Lieutenant Guse?"

"I do not. When I awoke the next morning, the door was broken and he was gone. My first thought was that the SS had come and taken him in the night. That was the reason for my visit the next morning."

"Your visit to the NSB office, on Hogestraat?"

"Correct."

"Can you describe what you found there, *bitte*?"

"On the second floor I found them all. The murdered NSB and Colonel Schmidt. The killer Hogeboom's cap and coat lay in the room."

"His cap and his coat?"

"Correct."

"How did you recognize these?"

"My men had arrested Hogeboom not long before. He was carrying radio equipment at the edge of this property, about to spy on us. I offered to spare his life if he'd work for Germany, and he agreed."

"On that first day, when you threatened Hogeboom with death, where exactly did you meet with him?"

"Here. In my office."

"Is it possible that anyone else might have seen the man here, wearing the cap or the coat?"

Erwin paused. "The woman gets occasional visits from friends, and from the Farm Inspector, but I don't think anyone came that day. I think I recall it was raining, so I doubt anyone would have been outside."

"Colonel Schell." Major Pelz leaned close, more earnest than ever. "Colonel Schmidt had interviewed Hogeboom also. Hogeboom gave Colonel Schmidt reason to suspect this Frau van Dordrecht worked for the Resistance. That much is clear from reports Colonel Schmidt sent."

Major Pelz leaned forward till his chest touched Erwin's desk. "And yet we find no record of these conversations in the local office."

Major Pelz wore a face of absolute trust, awaiting Erwin's reaction. Erwin's own face must have showed a blank. Major Pelz continued, "You understand the inference we draw?"

Erwin blinked.

"Whoever murdered Colonel Schmidt must have removed any records having to do with Frau van Dordrecht."

Brady returned from the hospital ship, still limping from the foot wound.

"Good morning, glories. Good to be back on dry land. I'm touring the company's position and you're my first stop. Surprised to see we're still so close to shore."

"The Brits were workin' Caen, so the western edge couldn't move without exposin' our flank,'" Haggerty answered. "After we did finally start, it's been slow goin.'"

"I heard the hedgerows were tough."

"They sure unloaded on us," Douglass started.

"We lost Green, Glass and Stringer the first day," Haggerty interrupted. "Stringer and Glass are dead. That's Stringer still on the other side that you smell."

Brady's face went deep red. "One day? You lost them all in one day?" Brady gripped the shorter Haggerty's shoulders and physically shook him. Then Brady spat and limped away. "Jesus Christ."

Thirty minutes later, Brady returned. "Sergeant, assemble your men."

Mad Jack Haggerty looked at the ground as he whistled up the men.

Brady's eyes moved from one man to the next. "I was out of line to blame Sergeant Haggerty. Every goddamned unit suffered in these hedgerows. Most of them worse than you. I don't know why the Army didn't plan for it. If it's anybody's fault here, it's mine. And if there's any sergeant who's good at keeping his men alive, it's Sergeant Haggerty."

In the silence, Willem knew what every man was thinking. Brady's shaking had humiliated their sergeant, and the public apology, no matter how Brady phrased it, only humiliated him again. But everyone knew that Haggerty would still report for duty at dawn the next day, and do what he had always done.

Willem was the first to speak to Brady. "By now Green's probably stable enough to evacuate. Want to visit him before he goes?"

"I'll join you," Douglass said. "If that's OK."

"Fine with me," Brady answered.

Willem and Douglass walked slowly so Brady could keep up, limping on his cane. The green medical tent, with its white circle and red cross, stretched over the sand. Just under the northern flap they found Green facing the water, writing in a spiral notebook.

Brady spoke first. "How you doin,' old-timer?"

"First day off morphine." His tone did not invite more conversation, and they all fell quiet again.

Brady chewed his finger, then spoke more to Willem and Douglass than to Green. "I forgot. On the hospital ship I got a report on Gilker."

"How is he?"

"Long way to go still. But listen to what he did: turned down a Purple Heart."

"What?"

"You know, right after the landing they needed some hero stories. In London some pretty high rankers went to his hospital to give him a Purple Heart, but Gilker turned them down."

Brady let a snort escape. "Gilker told them, 'Why honor someone for getting wounded? I was trying not to get wounded.'"

Green said, "That's stupid. Of course the medal's not for intentionally getting wounded. It's for taking more than his share of the pain we're all exposed to."

Douglass spoke up. "I think he understood that. And he'd still say pain's nothing to honor. Honor his accomplishments, if he had any; don't honor his sacrifice. That's what he meant."

"We've got it," Haggerty told the men next morning. "Line up, weapons ready."

A Sherman tank rumbled down the lane with pipes welded to its front. The tank thrust the explosive into the hedgerow and blew a wide hole. The tank inched forward into the opening, then fired a shell.

"White phosphorous," Haggerty said. "That should do it."

The tank's fifty-caliber gun raked the enemy hedgerow.

"OK," Haggerty said. "Douglass, keep a Browning Automatic hitting that opposite hedge. Everyone else follow the tank. Fire and movement, then grenades when you get close."

The squad followed the tank, using the ground, covering each other, sprinting and diving and firing to the opposite hedgerow, lobbing grenades. The tactics were unnecessary. Remnants of phosphorous still blazed on the hedgerow's brushy top, smoldering on a *Wehrmacht* body draped crazily over.

"There's one as met his Creator."

"Even water doesn't put it out," Haggerty said. "Once it's on you, you're cooked."

The squad cleared six squares that day, and twelve or more each day following, until at last they reached unbounded fields, the nightmare of hedgerow fighting suddenly over.

"The Nazis are retreating," Haggerty told the marching squad. "This is what Captain Brady talked about. Right now, they're close to being just a mob. We got to keep on 'em all the way to Germany, don't give 'em a chance to turn into an army again."

"'Keep up the skeer,'" Hall said.

Haggerty grinned. "Nathan Bedford Forrest."

"My namesake."

Airborne Jabos killed the German tanks. When the Germans retreated, the faster-moving Americans caught them. If the Germans stood and fought, the Americans went around them and cut them off. Absolute superiority, Willem thought: the way the Germans must have felt five years ago.

As the pace increased, he was able to think of Paardenveld again, without bitterness. It seemed the days of liberation, remarkable, historical days, would be over so soon he should keep a record. He began, euphorically, to write unsendable letters to Sophia.

Dear Sophia

> *In the last week we've marched through twenty towns. It seems we liberators are like a strong disinfectant. We see gaps in the row houses where artillery dislodged a section. Many of the buildings that survived have the inner brickwork or sheet-rock exposed. We're killing the invasion virus but we do a little scarring in the process.*
> *See you soon.*
>
> *Love,*
> *Willem*

He folded the unsendable letter and crammed it into his pack, the first of many.

Dear Sophia

> *We're still moving fast. This afternoon, marching next to Captain Brady, I said, "this is how joy would feel if you could actually touch it." He just nodded. Brady's my best friend, and had no idea what I meant.*
> *I wished I could speak to someone in Rhenen. No one else would understand what it feels like to be marching home.*
>
> *Love to you and Geertruide and Herbert*
> *Willem*

Even in July the brick street was cold to sit on as the men finished their coffee.

"Everybody!" Haggerty called. "Come where you can see me. Hightower, fire your M-1 that way." Haggerty pointed east, over the distant front line, where Hightower aimed his weapon and fired.

"Shoot again," Haggerty said.

Hightower fired once more.

"Keep shooting."

Hightower fired six more rounds, until the empty clip fell and clanged on the brick street.

"Did you hear that?" Haggerty asked. "Other squads tell me the Germans know how the M-1 works. After you empty a clip and it hits the street, the Germans hear it and know you're reloading. That's how they time their rush. So be careful. Expect a rush at the end of a clip. Movin' through villages you need to know this."

Ichinowski picked up an empty clip. "Watch." He pointed his M-1 at 45 degrees and fired eastward. Then his hand dropped the empty clip to the brick.

Haggerty's faced pumped. "Good! Everyone see what Ichinowski did? Carry an empty clip and drop it before the one in your gun is empty. They'll rush when you're still loaded. Ya see whud uh mean?"

Dear Sophia

Sometimes we march. Sometimes we ride in trucks when they're available. Gasoline is the only limiting factor. Brady says Patton's tanks drink gasoline faster than the Normandy ports can unload it.

By the roadside, men are re-painting trucks and jeeps. Winning makes very proud soldiers.

Normandy seems like a hundred years ago.

All my love,

Willem

In each town the French waved tiny American and British flags. They called to Willem, "Hey, Joe!" "Hey, Billy Yank!" Willem smiled and waved back. Once, after a French girl shouted "Joe!" he broke his marching cadence and tried a jitterbug he had seen Americans dance in England.

Dear Sophia

> *We take prisoners in growing numbers. More and more look either too young or too old for combat, a generation apart. All the mid-range of fighting age seem long gone. A lot are Ost-truppen: Hungarians, Rumanians, even captured Russians and Poles. These surrender quickly, as soon as the chance comes.*

> *Much love,*
> *Willem*

One afternoon the squad disabled a Panzer tank. Before anyone could put a grenade inside, the German crew scrambled out, hands high. With the surrender accepted, the Panzer crew relaxed.

"Look at those shit-eating grins," Hall said.

Lindell snorted. "Just what I was thinkin.' Those black Panzers scare you half to death, and who pops out? They look like boys you caught pullin' a prank. They smile at you, like you're supposed to see it was all a big joke."

Dear Sophia

> *Haggerty warns everyone now to steer clear of French jezebels. The warnings are wasted. The villages are producing fewer jezebels than the men would like.*
> *Don't worry about me.*

> *Love, Willem*

August, 1944

When Brady's company entered Paris, the happy delirium still lingered from its liberation four days earlier. Parisians were busy tearing down anything German: flags, insignia, Vichy government orders.

Brady ordered four days' leave.

Willem's parents had brought him to Paris when he was six, and he still had a six-year-old's memory of the wrought-iron balconies, the slow, uncomfortable dining in jacket and tie, the strange food his parents had loved.

On their honeymoon he had brought Sophia to stay at the Hotel Crillon, and had brought her again in the summer of 1939, just before Germany invaded Poland, to visit her brother Marc.

Dear Sophia

We marched down the Champs Elysees and through the Arche de Triomphe. Someone said we're making a show to intimidate the communists from the old Resistance.

If the Americans have found any reward for their efforts in Europe, they've found it here in Paris. The men throw chocolate, cigarettes, even C-rations into the crowds, and the crowds treat them like Hollywood stars. People thrust glasses of wine or cognac into the G.I.s' hands as they march. Women kiss them, maybe the closest the men will come to meeting Haggerty's jezebels.

Nearly everyone, even atheists, went to Mass at Notre Dame Cathedral. Standing room only.

Beneath the joy is a dark underside. In London, newspapers in 1940 wrote of "the rape of Paris." That's the right phrase. To think of the Paris occupation makes you think of a violated woman.

Tomorrow I'm going to see your brother.

Love,
Willem

The second day Willem woke early. He still remembered Marc's apartment on the Seine's Left Bank. Though Marc worked in the financial district, he spent his free time among the *artistes*.

Willem walked a kilometer to the Seine bridge. As he came in view of the apartment building, a surprising exhilaration ran through him. Marc was the nearest thing to seeing Sophia, and just a few steps away.

A woman swept the front steps.

"*Bonjour*," Willem offered. *"Je cherche mon beau-frere, Marc Lenoir."*

The woman stopped sweeping. *"Vous n'etes pas francais.* Who are you?"

"Willem van Dordrecht. *Hollandais.* You know Marc Lenoir?"

"Deported."

"Why?"

"Denounced as a Jew."

Willem clasped the woman's shoulders until he realized he was frightening her, and gently patted her arms. "What happened?"

"Someone tells the *milice* you're a Jew and away you go. I've seen the trains filling up, packed like cattle. No water, no food, no protection from the weather for a three-day, four-day journey."

The photographs in London showing white bodies in mass graves came back to Willem, the photographs smuggled out of Poland, the photographs that could have been his own family for all he knew, the photographs that had finally roused him from patience, the reasons he had left the London hospital to join the convoy escorts, then used every connection with Prince Bernhard to get posted in the units returning to France. The anger from those photographs came back, as he imagined Marc Lenoir one of those white murdered bodies. Marc, who today would have been his touchstone to Sophia.

"Who denounced him?"

"Oh, no one ever knows. But I would imagine it was Ricard, the concierge. See him in there, through that window."

In the ground floor apartment, a fat man with an old white shirt and a pinstriped vest rose and drew the curtains. Willem stopped listening and stared into the window, too angry to think.

"Do you have a key?"

"Only to the entryway."

"Can you let me in?"

The woman opened the building door, and Willem stepped to Marc's apartment. He jostled the doorknob but found it was bolted. He almost blew a shot through with his pistol to see if it would open. But why? What did he hope to find inside Marc's apartment? Instead he crossed the hallway and knocked on the concierge's door. No one answered and he knocked again.

From inside, "*Que voulez-vous?*"

"*Je suis le beau-frere de Marc Lenoir,*" Willem answered.

"*Et je suis occupé.*"

Busy! Willem unholstered his pistol and fired a shot into the lock. The man shouted from inside.

"Open the door!" Willem shouted.

"I'm trying! You broke it!"

Willem fired three shots in a row, then kicked the door open. Ricard the concierge stood just inside.

"You know my brother-in-law Marc Lenoir?"

The fat concierge nodded. "What about him?"

"Who denounced him?"

"*Sais pas.*"

Willem studied the man. "Did you ever denounce a Jew?"

"Who the hell are you?"

"Willem Vaubin van Dordrecht, attached to the American First Army. And I believe you denounced my brother-in-law."

"*Prouvez-le.*"

Willem froze. He saw again the joking killers in the photographs. How was the concierge any different, sending Marc to the trains? An unforgivable guilt, but of course the concierge would be gone by the time Willem could return to Paris for justice. An irresistible logic now moved him. He raised his pistol. The man cupped his hand over the barrel in self-defense but Willem squeezed the trigger, blowing a bullet at point blank through the palm, spattering blood and exposing the muscle. The wounded hand recoiled like a snake, and the concierge fell with a cry of pain onto his sofa.

Willem spoke like a judge. "Let's go tell the *gendarmes* what I've done and I won't deny it. If you're innocent, then I'm a criminal. They'll put me in prison for a long time. But if you denounced Marc, it will be in the records. Ready to go?"

The concierge wept with pain.

Willem waved his pistol. "I'm ready."

"I'm not going."

"Why not?"

The concierge gnashed his teeth from the pain of his hand. He stared out the window, and rocked in his pain. "Everyone denounced Jews!"

Willem felt his suspicion cool and solidify into certainty. What came next was automatic; no thought intervened between perception and action. He pointed his pistol at the man's face and fired but the man lurched backwards in fear, causing the bullet to hit his windpipe. The eyes widened, staring at Willem the way a still-living fish looks at a man who is cleaning it. The concierge gripped his own throat, gurgling then twitching as he slid against the armrest.

Outside in the open air, neighbors surrounded the sweeping woman.

Willem's hoarse voice sounded like someone else's. "The concierge denounced my brother-in-law. If anyone thinks I did wrong in killing him, I'll walk with you to the *gendarmes*. But I'll make sure you give a full accounting there too, for any denunciations you made." His voice grew louder. "Anyone challenge what I've done?"

"He deserved it," the sweeping woman answered. A few neighbors nodded. Others were silent, eyes accusing Willem. But no one accepted his challenge.

He walked again to the Seine. Ten blocks later came the full consciousness that he had just killed a weaponless man in cold blood. The fishlike face lived again in his mind as he looked at the pavement and dodged the other pedestrians without meeting their eyes.

Dear Sophia

I'm ready to leave Paris, push hard and get home. I feel like the only man not drinking at a wild party. And it is a wild party. Each morning, the smell of spilled wine and beer on the sidewalks, and urine in the alleyways, rises with the heat.

The joy of liberation here tells me the occupation was hard. It must have been hard for you. I'm ready to press on.

We're coming.
Willem

They assembled at 6 a.m. Willem looked at their faces, bleary and contented and sad, like his English friends the day after Christmas. He smiled. "I think I'm the only one ready to leave."

No one replied.

THE SOIL OF GELDERLAND
End of August, 1944

The men moved east away from Paris as rapidly as they had approached.

Brady spoke to Willem. "You've been so quiet. You okay?"

"Where are the British now?"

Brady sketched with a pencil. "Still just here. But we're moving fast."

"No one's moving fast toward Holland."

They marched again, silently until Willem spoke again. "Have you ever lived with only the future in mind? With no pleasure from the immediate? Four years ago, the future held no reality for me; now it's my only reality."

"At least you know what you want. So many people don't."

"The Germans are breaking down. I'm tempted just to desert and see how close to home I can get on my own."

Brady's eyes narrowed. "I understand the emotion. But what if every man did that? Then we'd just be an anti-German crowd instead of an Army. We'd still lose the war."

"I don't mean quite the same thing. Just go make sure they're safe, make arrangements, then rejoin." He looked at Brady. "It's not as if I haven't done my share."

"That doesn't change anything. You're either in or you're out. If you're in, you can't decide how much and where."

"If I sneaked off one night, would you try to stop me?"

"No. But I'd blame you. I'd say you took advantage of these men."

"I wonder what you'd do in my circumstances."

"I wonder that, too. But I'm not in your circumstances so it's easy for me to see it clearly." Brady clapped his hand on Willem's collarbone. "Willem, forget about your role as a soldier. Even for your own sake, I wouldn't recommend it. There are plenty of Germans all over western Europe, still full of fight. In your uniform, it would take a miracle to get through. And if you go as a civilian and they catch you, they'll certainly kill you. We can't help but win. It's all over but the misery. If your family's alive, they'll still be OK by the time you reach them. Do you think they'd rather see you sooner if it meant a higher risk of you getting killed?"

Willem looked away. "Four years."

"You think you're the only one?"

"You didn't know me when I left Holland. I look back at the way I was and wonder why my wife even loved me. She's a remarkable person. I'm not sure she'd say the same about me. To tell you the truth, I wonder if she's waiting for me."

"I'm telling you, you're not the only one. I've had men tell me stories like that as long as I've been in the Army. Willem, stay safe. We'll get there."

Willem marched quietly.

Brady cleared his throat. "The men trust you. I still need you to watch them for battle fatigue. After a long time in the field, soldiers sort of resign themselves to the idea of dying, as a way to make the dying less hard. That's when they get careless. The challenge is to keep them thinking dying's the worst thing, even though it increases the strain."

Douglass, Lindell and Hall began to talk of farming; others started to call them the Farmer's Club. Willem had never thought himself a farmer, but sitting with them at night brought Paardenveld back to him.

Hall said, "We rotated corn, tobacco and sweet potatoes. I wished Daddie would stick to corn, but we had to rotate. There is no work more unpleasant than sticking sweet potato slips, or tobacco plugs, or worming tobacco by hand. A farmhand was too expensive, so we boys did it.

"And you couldn't tell how the prices would hold after you planted. Our worst year, I believe it was '33, we sold the whole field of tobacco for forty dollars. I remember Daddie sittin' on the porch, holding four ten-dollar bills, just lookin' at me and laughin'. A real bitter laugh. He said, 'Not much for a year's work.'"

Lindell said, "I don't get the feelin' you were too happy on the farm."

"I'll tell you, there was a walnut tree right at the edge of our biggest field. Every morning I passed that tree on the way to a hard day in the heat. Then I'd pass it again comin' out. That tree, that never had to work a bit, it almost seemed it was laughin' at me. I'd tell it, 'just you wait. Someday I'll earn a livin' some easier way. And you will never see me again, tree.'

"Now, don't misunderstand me. I didn't talk to trees the way Indians do, like there's a spirit inside. It was more like a mirror. And every time I think my life is hard, I think about standing in that hot field, talking to that tree, and that's sort of my starting point. Anything I do's an improvement."

Douglass said, "Our farming's pretty different, mostly machines. We have four hundred acres and it's pretty flat. I just remember it being so, what's the word for it? Just . . . calm. It used to bother me, it felt so isolated. Now I think about it differently; it seemed like any danger in the world was only in the newspapers, a million miles away."

September, 1944

Sitting away from the others, Willem felt the crispening September air, remembered the odd elation the dry chill had used to evoke, and wondered why it no longer came.

Brady trudged to him, thumbs stuck in his pants waist. "Willem?"

Willem rose and followed Brady to his tent, the flap's canvas odor following him inside.

"Willem, this is Koos ter Horst, a Dutchman, in case you didn't guess. He'd like to speak with you alone."

Brady stepped out again through the tent flap.

"*Aangenaam*," the man said without expression.

"*Het zelfde,*" Willem said flatly. Did he recognize this man from the Queen's War Ministry in London, from the days before convoy duty?

"There's going to be a special push into Holland. It could end the war by Christmas. Would you like to be involved?"

"Of course."

"I can't tell you anything till after you've volunteered and we've left this place."

"I volunteer."

"Get your things. My jeep is just a hundred meters west on the road."

"I want to say goodbye."

"Don't say why you're leaving. You can only say it's a special assignment."

Willem strode into the little circle of Americans still unwounded: Ichinowski, Hightower, Hall, Douglass, and Lindell. His words came out like a laugh. "Well. I'm saying goodbye."

They stood. "Where are you going?"

"It's secret. Something closer to home."

"Closer to home?" Brady walked toward him. "That means something to get over the Rhine. If that's it, it could win the war." Brady put out his hand.

Lindell said, "Well, cabboy! Try to get us home for Christmas!"

Willem laughed. "If you get a chance, come to Rhenen before you leave. I'd love to see you at my home."

Haggerty put out a hammy shake. "If you're crossin' the Rhine somewhere, then most likely you're jumpin'." Haggerty inspected him. "The Flyin' Dutchman."

Hightower said, "Well, good luck then."

Now the September air brought again the old elation. Willem threw his duffle-bag into the back of Ter Horst's jeep, and jumped into the passenger seat as Ter Horst slung into gear and wheeled the jeep around toward the west.

Only now did Ter Horst begin to talk. "We'll drop airborne troops on bridgeheads over the Maas and the Waal in southern Holland, and over the Rhine at Arnhem. A British airborne division and a Polish brigade will hold Arnhem Bridge till a tank corps can link up from the Belgian border."

Ter Horst faced him. "Arnhem's so near your home, we thought you might like to join in. They'll need native speakers and you know the area. I should warn you, it involves a parachute jump."

"I'll need some training."

"You'll get it. Three mock jumps from a tower."

Willem scowled. "My first jump from a plane will be in combat?"

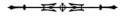

August, 1944

Dear Kolonel Schell:

>   *British air kept my company from reaching Normandy before the breakout. Now I lead a slow retreat across northern France. You can't imagine it: Ares moving unrestrained about our columns with the same bright fury he visited on the French in 1940.*
>   *British and American bombing destroys all rail transport. The pitiless fighter planes prevent daytime movement of the horse-drawn artillery. Ares' companions, Terror and Panic, light savagely about us.*
>   *My Ost-Truppen have no stomach for this. When I unsheath my sword it's not to fight the enemy, but to keep formation like*

an old-time corporal. I hide the troops from air attack and use them for deterrence, without letting them get close enough to find chances to surrender.

Growing numbers of French expose themselves to watch us retreat. They're not violent. But their hatred is undisguised. Long ago we watched newsreels of Austrians cheering the German soldiers entering Vienna. I never experienced such a welcome, not in Poland, not in the Netherlands, not here.

Approaching a village west of Paris, I saw crowds of French moving toward us, waving in ecstasy, hoisting long-hidden American flags. Then the French recognized our German uniforms, and hurried back indoors. A few scattered boys lingered unpoliced, staring, the way they might stare at a dying animal.

I remembered some reporter's phrase from 1940: "The Seine carries French blood to the sea, like the burst artery of a wounded man." Now I imagine German blood reddening the Seine.

I often imagine that you are suddenly here, taking control, wrong-footing the Americans, changing the momentum. I think of Guse, Kessler, Strohn, and Vogel. Even one of them at my side would change so much.

Sometimes I dream of the Dortmund brewery and its malt smell.

Perhaps we'll be together again soon.

Loyally,
Wolfgang Zimmer

Erwin folded it and looked out the window. No wonder Zimmer had sent the dispatch by hand. This was the letter of a man with his nerves shot. He imagined Zimmer with the haunted eyes he'd seen on so many soldiers in 1918.

Worse than the letter's desperate poetry, was its sheer pointlessness. Zimmer would never send something like this without an objective, unless he had lost control.

Erwin kicked a ball with Herbert, hoping the drizzle would not force them inside. His eyes stayed on the ball's spinning stitches, a rolling leather sphere of comfort and security.

Nothing was left of his recruiting. Since the Normandy breakout, no Netherlander expected Germany to win. No local had looked at him the same anyway, since the day he had carried the Jew from the square.

On clear days, he saw silver trails of V-1 rockets launched from Arnhem toward London, apparently a last desperate stroke of engineering malice. But Hitler's long-promised miracle weapon was surely too late. The German superiority of 1940 was gone, the best of its men and equipment squandered in too many battles on too many fronts over too many years, just as Langer and all the real fighters had warned.

Seyss-Inquart ordered German civilians to move east, near the German border. The Hollandish Nazi leader Mussert alerted party members to move east also. After the British captured Brussels and Antwerp, retreating German soldiers showed panic. Small groups of each -- the settlers, the local Nazis, the beaten soldiers -- passed Paardenveld on the river road, to escape the jams on the highway.

As the battlefront approached, tiny British reconnaissance planes flew under the low clouds, unchallenged with the *Luftwaffe* now devastated. Erwin never heard anti-aircraft batteries, and knew they saved their ammunition for combat planes.

Then the retreating soldiers began to regroup near Arnhem. General Student's airborne division, heroes of the invasion of Holland, inactive since the disaster at Crete, camped near Vught. Field Marshal Model made his new headquarters at Oosterbeek as he tried to exert Supreme Command in the West. Nearby, Bittrich's

Panzer Corps busily repaired itself. It seemed to Erwin they must be preparing for one last stand.

But still no one called him!

General Langer had not bothered to explain what was happening, and Erwin had not asked. If his country ever needed a soldier of Erwin's qualities, surely it was now. The *Wehrmacht's* failure to summon him could only mean the SS episode had clouded his career.

Now his only source of satisfaction was Sophia. But was there any way to be sure of her? Her affection for him had too many selfish motives: protection from the SS, security from going without, and a father figure for her children.

He could not remember when he had last felt the old sense of mission, and he could not remember when the painfulness had first replaced it. The vague pain, living placelessly inside him, had been his companion so long, he was actually comfortable with it.

As he had become accustomed to the painfulness, taken it for granted, he had also begun to imagine the cool metallic taste of a pistol barrel in his mouth, then the splintering of his skull from the discharge, releasing his trapped spirit from pain. The cool metallic taste of the pistol barrel had come to him every day for as long as he could remember now, and it did not shock or frighten him. The cool barrel in his mouth, and the release that would follow, had begun to seem the most natural thing in the world.

Only a Homeric second image blunted the pistol barrel's lure: the image of Hektor's dead body dragged in disgrace below the walls of Troy. Now, when Erwin tried to imagine his own funeral, he imagined the burial of a disgraced soldier, forgotten by his country. Release was an illusion.

The spinning ball moved toward him, and he took a momentary comfort in kicking it and watching it roll toward Herbert.

On the river road a German soldier walked with a familiar step. Now Erwin lost awareness of the ball as Herbert chased it. The German was Wolfgang Zimmer, staring ahead like a hunted animal. Erwin trotted toward him and embraced him like a son.

"What happened? Where's your detachment?"

"Many killed, the rest taken prisoner at the end."

"Does your commander know where you are?"

"No. I'm missing in action." Zimmer's face twitched as he spoke, and he looked away in shame.

"You're shell-shocked. Stay here till you're recovered. You can rejoin your regiment later."

The broad glass panes moaned in the September wind. Anna watched Geertruide and Herbert play checkers on the sewing-room floor while Sophia needle-pointed a dish warmer.

"Jan's a prisoner of war again," Anna said. "With the British at the border, the Germans are re-arresting paroled officers."

"Surely they'll treat him well enough, with the end so near," Sophia answered. "How's Roos?"

"Bitter. You know her, Sophia. She's not philosophical."

Sophia almost asked whether Roos spoke of her, but stopped and said instead, "Well, then we're all war widows again, with Jan a prisoner, Maarten in a labor crew, and Willem in France."

"In France! How do you know that?"

Sophia almost told her everything: the chapel radio and *el tio* messages, the Farm Inspector, her theft of Colonel Schussler's letter.

She stopped herself. The time would come, but not yet. Instead she said, "Where else would Willem be?"

"Maybe we'll see him first. Sophia, what a thrill for you!"

"But have you noticed, Anna? The Germans are slowing in this area, as if they plan to defend it."

In the chapel Sophia listened to Radio *Oranje* with the children. Through the static came Holland's national anthem, the *Wilhelmus*.

From London Queen Wilhelmina declared that victory was near, with British troops in Antwerp just south of the Belgian border. Wilhelmina named Prince Bernhard Commander-in-Chief of "the Netherlands Forces."

Thirty-three-year-old Prince Bernhard took the microphone, urging resistance groups to prepare armlets "displaying in distinct letters the word '*Oranje*,'" but asking them not to use the armbands "without my order." Now a military band played *Oranje Boven*.

Sophia watched the children's reaction as the American General Eisenhower spoke next. "The hour of liberation the Netherlands have awaited so long is now very near."

At the air base in Gloucestershire, bottle-nosed C-47's lined the runway like drab dolphins with wings. Willem put the terror of jumping out of his mind.

Airborne, the terror seized him again. Only the thought of touching home soil calmed him. In two hours his feet would hit the broad, flowered *Ginkelse Heide* he had passed so many times on his bicycle. How long would it take the British tanks to reach them? Two days? Three?

"Who packed these parachutes?" an English jumper asked.

"Your sister, your wife, your mother. It's all women at the packing tables."

"If it was my wife, I don't like our chances! Trade me?"

Their dark humor faded in Willem's awareness. Life was beginning again, a reunion with Sophia, as precious as his wedding day.

As the C-47 crossed the coastal batteries of North Holland, flak began to explode around it. Willem braced against the plane's evasive twisting, choked down his airsickness and thought again of the Gelderland heaths.

"Line up!"

Willem was fifth. The line moved so quickly there was no time to panic or reconsider. At the jump-master's cue, Willem pushed himself out the open door. The air hit like a solid object, pulling him away from the fuselage as if the C-47 were standing still, and he was swimming away in whitewater rapids of air. He felt an alien weightlessness, then with relief felt gravity's downward tug.

His chute cord pulled automatically from the static line, making a loud pop as the strapping nearly dislocated his lowered shoulder. It felt as if the chute were anchored in something solid, pulling him away from the ground. Looking instinctively upward, he saw his chute billow wide, tangle-free and perfect.

The ground lay half a kilometer below. Bursts of orange and puffs of black smoke marked the German gunnery's response. Every parachutist steered as best he could toward the heath they recognized from maps. But a clutter of bullets made a chug-chug against the canvas of Willem's chute. Looking up, he saw enormous holes in the canopy. He fell faster and straighter, separating from his jump-mates and reaching a dangerous drop speed.

The earth leapt up and hit him from below, spraining both ankles. Pain rocketed up past his knees. He barked in pain and then lay still. He could see the *Ginkelse Heide* just a few hundred meters to the north, but could not see his jump-mates. The ankle pain warred in his brain with the exultation of touching Gelderland soil, and he found himself grasping little clumps of turf.

A pair of tall *Wehrmacht* riflemen, with weapons ready, trotted up to him. They looked nearly fifty years old. Willem put his rifle aside and kept his hands off the ground, thinking bitterly of his failed homecoming, with no idea what kind of treatment to expect. He waved a pack of Camel cigarettes from his pack.

"*Wollen Sie Sigaretten? Chocolade?*"

The Germans smiled as they fingered the Camels and the chocolate bar. "*Sie sprechen gut Deutsch!*"

Willem remembered his British uniform, and understood their surprise at his German.

"*Ich bin niederlander,*" he told them.

"*Niederlander?*" The Germans looked at each other and patted his shoulder. The cigarettes and chocolate seemed unnecessary; there seemed no slaughter in these two. Willem imagined that they thought the war lost, even that they wished he were capturing them, ending their danger.

"We'll take you to the hospital near Rhenen," one said.

Near Rhenen? Willem wondered if they meant his old clinic, Sint Anna.

The two Germans interlocked their arms to make a chair and carried him to the road, where one trotted off to get a vehicle, leaving the other with Willem.

Soon the departed German returned on a motorcycle. They lifted him gently into the sidecar, helping him place his feet to avoid pain. The second German straddled the seat behind the driver.

They rode west to Veenendaal, then south toward Rhenen, passing Paardenveld. Willem almost asked them to stop. He stared at the house and lawn, seeing no one.

At Sint Anna, an attendant brought out a wheelchair. Only the shooting pains marred his elation as he scanned the white coats for Maarten. Where was his partner?

They wheeled Willem to an empty bed. Gripping the bedrail, he noticed his left hand still held the clump of *gelderse* soil.

Maarten never came. A German doctor with birth-marked hands set Willem's ankles.

Willem called an orderly to his bedside. *"Kennen Sie Paardenveld?"*

"I can speak English," the orderly said. "Yes, I know Paardenveld. It's a training center. The colonel in charge married the owner's widow."

"We're leaving in thirty minutes," Erwin told Zimmer and Nagel. "British paratroopers are at Arnhem. An armored thrust is moving up from Eindhoven to meet them. We'll reconnoiter for river crossings downstream."

This assignment was perfect for rebuilding Zimmer's confidence. Nagel was not his ablest fighter, but perfectly reliable. Searching for his long-unused combat gear, Erwin felt relief, finally to be needed.

At Sint Anna's, Willem lost his bed to the more severe cases, now crowding in. He slept on a floor mat, and during daylight he sat against the wall.

One of his jump-mates from the C-47 was carried in, missing one hand. The man recognized Willem. "We landed in the middle of a bleedin' Panzer division," he said. "And still no contact with Thirty Corps."

"No contact, even by radio?"

"All the radios are useless. This is a bleedin' disaster. A bleedin' disaster."

Three volunteer nurses walked through the door, their clothes still shiny from the drizzle. Willem saw Anna Meurs before she saw him.

He found himself deadpanning to control his emotion. *"Dag, Mevrouw Meurs. Hoe gaat het met U?"* But his emotion came through, and the joke in his voice gave way to a sound almost like begging.

Anna jumped, then stepped closer, until suddenly she knew him. "Willem!" Then, longer and more loudly, "Willem! Oh, Willem!" Anna knelt and pulled him against her shoulders. She ran her fingers though his dirty hair, as if he were her own husband.

Willem trembled as he spoke. "Anna, what are you doing here?"

"We knew the British were struggling. We wanted to help in some way." She pulled away and passed her hand over his balding scalp. "Willem, what are you doing here?"

"They thought locals like me could help with directions and communication. But my parachute tore, and I landed too hard. Where's Maarten?"

"He's in a labor crew, building defenses. Free soon, I hope." Anna studied his face. "You look so different!"

"Anna, tell me about Sophia and Geertruide and Herbert."

"Willem, they're fine. A German colonel made a training center at Paardenveld. He let them all stay home, and he makes sure they're safe. He even plays *voetbal* with Herbert. Oh, Willem, they're fine. I'm leaving now to tell them you're here. Sophia will want to come right away and see you."

He held her. "Anna, stay one more minute."

"Yes, Willem?" He saw from her face he was alarming her. "What is it?"

"Has Sophia married the German colonel?"

"Are you joking? What makes you ask such a thing?"

"One of the orderlies told me."

"That's ridiculous. The colonel's men protected your family, and yes, they are friends. But Sophia knew you were alive. She's told me." Anna leaned close. "Willem, Sophia speaks constantly of you."

He nodded, still uncertain.

Anna pushed away again. "Willem, I must go tell her."

Thirty minutes passed.

Willem tried to imagine his family now. Would Geertruide thrill to see him? Would Herbert even know him? Had Sophia fallen in love with the German colonel? He must look so beaten up; it was the first time he could remember worrying about his looks.

Anna came through the door first, then stopped and looked back. Why was Sophia so far behind? Then, just outside the doorway, he saw her. Anna gestured toward Willem with a smile.

He watched Sophia's face as she searched his to the point of recognition. Then he saw Sophia's eyes crinkle into her irresistible smile. Sophia ran to kneel beside him; she put her hands on his face, and then the hot skin of her cheeks met his own.

Sophia tried to joke. "*El tio no esta infermo.*"

Willem chuckled through his tears. "*El tio se ha vuelto.*"

She leaned back to see him, holding his hands, then kissed him, then moved back again. "Willem, Willem, Willem."

Each of them stroked the other's face and hair and hands.

"Willem, your father died just after the invasion."

"The defense ministry in London got word, and let me know. He was a remarkable man, wasn't he?"

Sophia nodded. "He died in his sleep."

"You know, people here always treated me well because of my father. I remember – in fact I thought about this a lot while I was away – I remember the times after dinner when he used to bring me here to check on patients. I must have been six or seven years old, no more. I was too young to go into the hospital rooms, so I read cartoons on that long bench in the waiting room. Even then, he already limped from ruining his knee in field hockey, and the hard soles of his shoes made that syncopated clap against the hallway floor. That's how I knew he was coming to get me. It was the friendliest sound I could remember: the sound of my father coming."

Sophia smiled her irresistible smile.

"When I was in medical school, there was a day when I thought it was just too much. I told him it was the hardest thing I had ever done. My father answered, 'You can do anything you set your mind to.' He didn't say it like a homily, but as a specific observation he had made about me, his son. I never looked back again, and finished second in the class."

Sophia nodded, imagining their conversation and drinking it in.

"Sophia, when your father was dying, flush with morphine, only half-conscious, still stammering with pain, I asked my father, 'What can be worse than cancer?' Did I ever tell you what he answered?"

Sophia shook her head, smiling inquisitively.

"Fear of cancer."

She released a little breath of a laugh.

"My life was easy because of my father. He never shouted at me, always listened, always made me feel that everything would be all right, actually that everything already was all right." Willem stopped smiling, and looked intently at Sophia. "Did I show him the respect he deserved? A lesser man would have asked more from his son."

"Willem, Willem."

They were quiet for some time.

"Your mother died also, just last May. Did you know that also?"

"My mother? No, that's impossible. How could a woman like that not live forever? My God." He paused. "My God. Sophia, did you ever meet more humanity in a single person? She was a hundred people in one. If I think about all the color in my childhood . . ." He sounded ridiculous, even to himself . . . "It was as if it all radiated from her."

"I know exactly what you mean. That's a perfect way to say it. No, I never met more humanity in a single person."

"What happened?"

"She never was the same after your father died. She just deteriorated and then finally died. They're both buried at Paardenveld: I'll show you when you can walk. I think Colonel Schell can arrange your release, if you agree to become a civilian."

"I'm not ready to become a civilian until the Germans are beaten and gone," he said softly.

"We can talk of that later. I'll bring the children tomorrow. It will be the happiest day of their lives."

The next morning Willem woke at four o'clock, full of adrenaline to see his children. By a quarter to eight, the day already seemed half over; then Sophia appeared at last in the doorway. Willem craned to look past her at the children. There was Geertruide, nearly as tall as Sophia but thinner. Herbert looked around in puzzlement like a miniature man.

Geertruide recognized him first, running and hugging him with her little-girl arms. "Poppy!" Geertruide, the knowing one. She still had the same clear, gray eyes.

Herbert put his hand out stiffly to shake. Willem pulled the boy forward and held him close, and knew again the leather-grain sweet smell of Herbert's skin, the same as his baby days. But Herbert was stiff and restrained.

Geertruide asked, "Are your legs going to get better?"

"We'll be skating together by winter." Willem tried to sound cheerful but his voice came out like a dirge. "Let me just look at you."

The next morning Sophia wore the white skirt and blouse of a volunteer, and brought a little pot of boiled apples. "There's hardly any food now, mainly apples and potatoes. These have a little cinnamon, anyway, from the pantry."

Willem squeezed her hands. "Sophia, I've seen so much since I left, shattered families, children with desperate, haunted faces."

His lips quivered. "Not our children. Not ours. Not with their extraordinary mother, who kept their little souls intact."

Sophia began to cry.

"Excuse me." The German doctor appeared. "Am I interrupting?"

Willem looked at the man and thought, of course you're interrupting, just look at her. "No," he answered. "What can we do for you?"

"You're a surgeon, aren't you?"

"Yes."

"We've lost two doctors, and we have orders to merge the medical staff here to the regional hospital in Arnhem. But casualties are rising and we'll still have to bring overflow here. I'm wondering if you will lead the staff that stays behind."

"I can't stand up. I think I could sit on a high chair to operate."

"It may be awkward, but otherwise we'll have to neglect some patients. Even with you helping, we won't meet the total need."

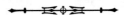

Sophia was there at the end of the surgery. Willem looked exhausted, content to let Sophia scrub his forearms, sagging with fatigue.

"I remember back when I started with surgery, in those earliest days, the first time I saw the red-white marbeling of a man's lung without nausea, instead with a kind of competence, maybe even smugness, as if I'd joined some tiny elite with a secret code, with a kind of mastery over the messy tissue.

"That seems so long ago. Now the feeling of power is different: it's knowing I can extend a soul's visitation in this world. When I open a body now, I think of the mind."

"I love you, Willem."

"The first year I was away, I thought of your face, your hair, your skin, the way it felt to lie next to you. Then those images faded, and I remembered your soul. I'd lost my soul's companion. I knew the thing I wanted most was to finish my soul's visitation in this world with yours."

"He's different, isn't he, Sophia?"

How like Anna to notice. "Yes, Anna," Sophia answered. "He's changed."

And how like Anna to leave it at that, not to intrude further into her thoughts as they walked past the western gate.

It was more than the baldness that reached halfway to the back of his scalp, the shallow beard, the deepening creases that ran away from his eyes, the leathery skin. It was a new steadiness. Willem looked at her as if conscious of no one else, instead of the half-distracted way he had before the war, his mind wandering ahead to the next bicycle race, the next dinner party, the next Leiden reunion. Now his gaze seemed almost tangible, as if it could physically bridge the space between them, uncompromised by any half-smile or a clever word.

She remembered her earliest feelings for the handsome young student, popular but less arrogant than his friends, his nobler name, his humbler airs. She remembered the early, elemental years of their marriage and the births of their children. These old images mingled with the new face of the man in the hospital, mature and purposeful.

"Sophia," he had said to her in the hospital.

"Yes?" she had answered.

"I was gone a long time. I . . ."

"Tell me."

"In many ways, I wandered."

"In many ways, you didn't," she had answered.

It was not until the fourth day that he told her. "Sophia, your brother Marc was deported."

"Deported? When?"

"I'm not sure. A cleaning woman at his apartment building told me."

"For labor?"

Willem wavered. "The concierge told the *milice* he was Jewish."

Jewish. Marc's letters: the heritage he said she had disowned. Jewish. Jew. The word repeated itself in her mind until it dissolved into a non-word, into sound unrooted to any meaning. Jewish. Jew. Jewish. Jew.

"It shocked me," Willem said.

Shocked him. Or had Willem sensed a foreignness about her before, a foreignness that she hid from herself? The reason his mother seemed cold on their first meeting? The reason he'd fled from her so many times after they married, as if to be with her any length of time were more than he could stand?

She barely heard Willem continue. "Someone calls him Jewish and he's gone. I've never imagined anything like it."

He'd never imagined. Maybe Jews had imagined it, the climax of a thousand-year nightmare. All the conversions to Christianity, the hunger for success and acceptance, had it all been some collective premonition of the holocaust now unfolding? Like a flock of frightened helpless birds, fluttering in unison against a change in the wind that brought the predator's scent?

Had she known all along, half-conscious of the signs and turning away from them? Her father's shrug and change of subject whenever asked about the past, her own rush into a *jonkheer* marriage, enfolding herself in a Christian church whose religion she never believed, her reach for Colonel Schell's protection when Roos would have spit on him and left Paardenveld: did it all mean that in her deepest subconscious she had known, and sought her own refuge, less brave than the most pitiful bird in the flock, deserting her species even as it fled?

"I'll find Marc when this is over," Willem said. "Sophia, you look as if you're in shock. I'm telling you, I'll find him."

SEPARATIONS
Early October, 1944

The British airborne operation was defeated. British tanks had reached the near approaches, but Arnhem Bridge and all the Rhine remained in German hands. The front was stable again.

Erwin's depression returned. Defeat still yawned in a widening grin of certainty. All the Myrmidons were gone except the nerve-shattered Zimmer. General Langer knew Erwin was idle, and still offered no combat posting.

Sophia had become distant. Had the nearness of liberation made it unnecessary for her to pretend?

These thoughts seemed to make his head and body heavier as he leafed through his mail. He found a note from General Langer.

Unsealing the envelope, he unfolded an invitation to the General's headquarters. At last, surely a combat assignment.

He rose before dawn, polished his shoes, and put on his full uniform and medals. "I'm going alone," he told Nagel. "I'll drive myself."

The flat, watery fields gave way to rolling hills that grew steeper and more wooded as Erwin moved the car southeast. Driving, he began to feel the old purpose and happiness he always felt in General Langer's presence.

He arrived in four hours. In the front yard, enormous red Nazi banners drooped against two polished steel poles, lifted occasionally by short gusts. He pulled into the driveway and turned off the engine, checking his uniform as he stepped out. His boot soles crunched into the tiny gravel of the driveway, until he stepped onto the soft lawn.

Just after the doorbell, Langer's adjutant Captain Sinder greeted him. Each man knew of the other's closeness to General Langer, and they had always shared a mutual regard. Today Sinder showed less energy than usual, but was still polite. "I think he's ready to see you, Colonel. I'll tell him you're here."

When General Langer appeared, he extended a hand and looked at Erwin's face with the old admiration. No one made Erwin feel more sure of himself.

General Langer gestured toward the door. "It's so beautiful today, why don't we take a walk?"

"Certainly."

"Captain Sinder, can you have something ready when we return?"

"*Jawohl, Herr General.*"

General Langer's age limited their walking pace. Erwin waited for his mentor to speak first, but the General took longer than usual to begin, and seemed content just to walk together. Finally Erwin asked, "You have news from Berlin?"

"I spoke with Rommel very recently. I think I told you, perhaps I did not, last July, Von Rundstedt advised Hitler to make peace. That's why Hitler removed Von Rundstedt from command in the West, why Field Marshal Model, with no combat experience, led the defenses near you until von Kluge replaced him recently."

They walked a little farther. "Yes, I've spoken with Rommel very recently." Langer pinched his face forward. "Erwin, you know of the assassination attempt against Hitler, last summer in East Prussia? The briefcase with a bomb?"

"I heard something about it. I'd put it out of my mind."

"Some of the highest ranks were involved. A Colonel Claus Graf von Stauffenberg placed a briefcase bomb near Hitler in a meeting, then excused himself. But someone moved it, and it injured Hitler only slightly. Graf von Stauffenberg's involvement was obvious. He's been executed, after a long interrogation. Five thousand people, including conspirators' families, executed so far. Von Kluge took poison."

"What about Rommel?"

"He was recovering at home from a wound when his involvement became known. Hitler would be embarrassed for the public to know that a hero like Rommel was against him. So Hitler gave Rommel the option of taking poison, to avoid a public trial. Rommel will take it."

They walked in silence until General Langer finally asked, "Enough walking for you? Perhaps Captain Sinder will have something ready for us."

"Certainly."

General Langer was quiet again as they retraced their steps.

At last he said, "Erwin, I also knew. There have been so many interrogations, it's only a matter of time before I'm found out. I don't wish to be interrogated." Langer paused, but only for a moment. "Sinder will give me poison this evening. Tomorrow the newspapers will say I died of a heart attack."

Erwin could not have been more shocked if General Langer had struck him with the back of his hand. He gripped the old man's shoulders as if to brace him, but actually he was bracing himself. A passing car slowed, as if to see if something were wrong. General Langer patted Erwin's arms and resumed walking.

"Erwin, the war is over. The Americans have unbelievable strength. They produce weapons and equipment faster than we could destroy them, even if we fought them constantly and won every battle. They're not the best soldiers, but they're good enough to stay in the war and win it. American planes fly unchallenged. They have strategic superiority in the same way that we had in the earliest days."

They passed a woman cleaning a brick walkway, the cleanser's odor keen in Erwin's nostrils.

"Think also of the Russians. This is precisely what the General Staff always wanted to avoid, the one certain way to lose the war. Hitler let it happen.

"If we'd stopped the Normandy invasion, the Americans might have turned to the Pacific, and there might have been a chance. That won't happen now.

"Hitler will never surrender. In his perverted *Führer* thought, Germany is no longer separate from him; he cannot fall without Germany destroyed.

"The kindest thing we can do for Germany is to let the British and Americans enter Berlin peacefully, before they destroy it with their bombing. Before the Russians come in."

They reached the house, and General Langer opened the front door. Their boots echoed on the floor as they strode to a little study.

General Langer gestured to a chair. "*Bitte.*" They both sat.

"Because of your close association with me, you'll be a suspect. But I don't think the Gestapo will take active measures against the rank of colonel, at least not colonels in the field, with no direct involvement. As long as Hitler stays in power, you won't advance. But you shouldn't be in danger."

Sinder brought in a tray with two brandy snifters, two water glasses, a decanter of cognac, and a crystal pitcher of cold water. General Langer interrupted Sinder's service and handed Sinder one of the empty water glasses, pouring some cognac into it. "You drink with us, too," the General told his adjutant. General Langer then filled Erwin's snifter and his own. He stood very straight and held his snifter. Erwin quickly stood up also.

"I thought my final toast would be to the Fatherland, or some commemoration of my services to Deutschland. Instead, I raise a glass to two of the finest men I've had the privilege of working with. My respect and affection for you both knows no limits."

The men clinked glasses. Erwin and Sinder acknowledged the General's salute only by their expressions, because to reply would have been disrespectful. Erwin could look directly at Langer for only an instant. Instead he looked down and drank his cognac in one slow swallow.

Sinder refilled Erwin's and Langer's snifters, left the decanter, and carried out the tray. General Langer gestured toward Erwin's chair, inviting him to sit again.

"I was unable to contact Colonel Schussler. You'll say something to him, I hope, something to communicate my esteem for him."

"Of course."

General Langer grimaced as he continued. "Erwin, you are extraordinarily capable, and you'll find challenging work in civilian life. Germany will be rebuilding and need competent men, with so many of the finest dead. You have the chance to learn from our mistakes. You and I have both existed for our country, first for Imperial Germany and the Kaiser, then for Weimar." He laughed without mirth. "Then for the Third Reich.

He leaned close to Erwin. "You can be the first of us to exist for yourself."

One hand on the steering wheel, Erwin shuffled in the leather seat. He had said goodbye forever to the noblest German he had ever known. He thought of their long mountain walks, their excited discussions of strategy as they lost track of the time. He thought of the opportunities the old man had placed before him and, he realized now, the risks General Langer must have taken to protect him. General Langer must have felt for a very long time that the war could not be won. That must have been the same time Langer quit finding combat roles for Erwin.

Most of all, Erwin thought of Langer as the great example, the wonderful teacher, and the best symbol of German idealism. Taking poison tonight.

Erwin was not part of a Thousand-Year Reich, connected spiritually to the heroes of mythology. He was part of a shameful scheme run by hoodlums and psychopaths, the molesters and plunderers he had always been sure he was not.

Germany could never go to war again. And Germany at peace would have no need of sacrifice or heroism. The more he considered peacetime Germany, the more the idea disturbed him. He thought of the Germans who lived civilian lives, though he had never known any well. He imagined himself as shopkeeper, selling for his own account. What was it that made life seem unthinkable without heroic sacrifice, without the World's attention and sanction?

He thought of his earliest memories, sitting in the church pew at Christmas, first the soloist singing "O Holy Night," then the choir singing "Silent Night," the solemn faces of all the girls, including his older sister who was beautiful and wise and made him feel dirty and incompetent. All were devoted to the Christ child, who had sacrificed himself for them all. They all worshipped little Jesus' purity of spirit, sanctified his altruism, this Christ child who was so unlike little Erwin. He had felt rage and envy then and thereafter for Jesus, the great sacrificer, the only boy worthy of all these girls Erwin adored.

He thought of the quotes he had put on the blackboard for his officer classes, from Kant "the principle of one's own happiness is the most objectionable of all" and self-love "the very source of evil."

In the First World War, Erwin had won the greatest military glory Germany could award. He had also nearly died. What had he gained fighting in the trenches, other than the State's recognition? Who was the State? How many actual Germans even knew what he had done? How many cared?

He thought of his triumphs in Poland and Holland. How had he gained from them? How had anyone gained, even the people putting the medals on him?

The Nazis had destroyed so many lives, misdirected so many German minds, including his own. No, he thought. The Nazis had not misdirected his mind. He had allowed it to be misdirected, had even misdirected it himself. During his entire adult life, his reason had slumbered, and his only purpose had been the approval of others. He scowled to think of his mindlessness, a mindlessness that had lasted even till this morning, when it had still taken General Langer to show him the way.

What about Sophia? Was this really love at all, or had she only replaced the German *Volk* as the mirror of his own worth? He recalled the thrill when Sophia seemed to approve of him, all the times he felt empty and anxious to change her mind when she showed anything less.

He pulled the car onto the road's gravel shoulder, walked into the trees, sank to his knees and sobbed. He wondered if he could stand the emptiness of life without his career, wondered if it were possible to change from the man he had just come to despise.

He lost track of time. Cars rumbled past, but the drivers paid no attention to him; it was not unusual now to see a German officer with his nerves gone, behaving strangely.

Finally he returned to the car, unfastened his sword and scabbard from his belt and laid it in the passenger seat. He drove in silence. Now the gray cloth of his uniform seemed a badge of servitude, like a waiter's red jacket. He yearned to have it off, to know the freedom of civilian clothing, to be spontaneous and unmarked.

Paardenveld came into view. As he turned into the gravel driveway, the sword careened left and brushed his pants. He pushed it back into place as the car crept to the house. "The sword! I'll never lift the sword again except to defend my own conscience." He spoke aloud, as if someone could hear.

Sophia searched for the words she could use with Erwin.

She felt as if she were waking from a blurred dream. The two essential clarities had returned: first, that life is short, and second that only she was capable of creating her own happiness. For a desperate time, these clarities had forsaken her and she had surrendered her self-responsibility to a protector, a father.

That was finished. The idea she might love Erwin Schell had been a lapse, a salve whose curative powers vanished with the disease. Erwin had been her knight in the Dark Ages, but the Dark Ages were over. Willem's sudden return restored the two clarities, vital for real love.

To prolong things with Erwin would be shameful. But every script she rehearsed sounded humiliating.

"Sophia . . ."

She cringed when she heard Erwin call from the front door. As he stepped into the sewing room, she rose reflexively, and wished she could run away.

"Sophia . . ."

"What is it?" she asked, still racing to think how she could tell him.

"I need to tell you something."

"What is it?" she asked again.

"Sophia . . . I need to separate from you awhile."

Did he know about Willem? "What's wrong?" she asked.

"Will you sit down? Please."

She sat in the sewing chair. Erwin pulled up a child's stool and took her hand.

"Sophia . . . I am looking back at my time here . . . with a new clarity. I see myself, I see myself with you . . . Let me start again. Looking back, I think that I loved you the moment we met, and then I loved you more every time some little thing happened that let me know you better. The night we first made love was the greatest joy in my life."

She studied his face for a sign where this was leading.

"But . . . something has happened. I can't fully explain it, but suddenly I . . . see myself very differently. Suddenly I'm not sure that I trust anything that I've ever believed, or anything that I think I know or feel. I . . . I don't know what to do except to start over. To separate myself from everything I've depended on, then see what comes back naturally, after I've changed."

"What's happened?"

Erwin drew a deep breath. "Ever since I can remember, I've lived for approval." He looked at the floor. "In fact, I'm not sure I ever lived for anything else. The approval of others, people I don't even know, people who don't even know me, no better than a stripper in a cabaret."

He paused, so long that she wondered if he were finished. Then he said, "More and more, I think, for yours."

He looked at her as if to make sure there was no ambiguity. As if the notion that he wanted her approval somehow perverted every bond between them.

"I have to find out if I can live without anyone's sanction, to see how that feels. Our friendship started with wanting your approval. I need to get away from you, and then know whether I still love you, for the right reasons.

"And if I still love you, I'll want to be sure you love me. I won your love dishonestly by living for you, by hiding my real self. It worked perfectly, because even I was fooled. The best liars are always the ones who can fool themselves.

"When that's gone, I want to know if you can love me in the way you loved your husband."

Sophia kept quiet. There were so many things she might say. But now the best thing was to say nothing.

In his office, Erwin still felt empty and tired. A new letter from Colonel Schussler sat for two days before Erwin finally unsealed it.

> *Dear Erwin,*
>
> *The Russians have crossed the Vistula outside Warsaw. We lose whole army divisions at a time. I have little hope the Russians will show any mercy, and I will fight to the death.*
> *You and I have always done our utmost for the Fatherland. Together we lived through the bleak years, then through majestic triumphs. I am not a religious man. My life in arms has been my sacrament, our comradeship my communion.*
> *One thing I know is that I will maintain my honor. I wish you honor also, to the end.*
>
> *Yours,*
> *Horst Schussler*

It was unbelievable that such a letter had gotten through. Even the censors must have been called away from their desks to stop the Russians!

Erwin looked out the window, imagining Schussler's predicament. At best, surrender meant a Russian labor camp. After the *Einsatzgruppen* murders, his captors would not be kind.

Erwin thought of the men he had lost. Guse. Vogel. Strohn. Probably Kessler. General Langer. Now Colonel Schussler. The letter reminded him how strong was the lure of honor and sacrifice. But Schussler was not a part of him now. He felt a chill, as if he were loose in space.

On Monday, Erwin faced the window, his back to his desk, wearing only his pants, his undershirt and suspenders.

"Colonel Schell," Nagel intoned from behind. "The SS Major is back." Erwin wheeled distractedly, to see Major Pelz enter with an aide and close the door.

Pelz spoke with the reverence he might give his own commanding officer. "Colonel Schell, I'm confident enough of the Hollandish woman's guilt to arrest her. Out of respect, I'm notifying you before making an arrest on your grounds."

Erwin put his finger over his mouth to suggest silence. Major Pelz's eyes pinched earnestly. Erwin gestured toward the walls and ceiling, then pointed to his ear to show a suspicion of listening devices.

"Major Pelz, will you come on a short walk? I have some information that should interest you a great deal."

The major nodded conspiratorially.

Erwin put on his tunic, then reached for his holstered pistol and draped the belt over his shoulder. "Let's go."

Behind the house their boots crunched acorns as they passed the oak table and crossed the little canal bridge. Erwin led them down the dirt track that bordered the woods.

"Major Pelz, I share your suspicions. This woman has so many visitors. I suspect the Farm Inspector -- is that your theory too?"

Pelz smiled and nodded. "Exactly."

At the fork in the track, Erwin gestured left toward the path into the wood. He looked back to check whether they were being watched.

"I've found something that should prove your case, Major."

He led them down the left path, then pulled aside some overgrowth and faced the two SS men. "It looks like solid ground, *ja?*"

Major Pelz and his aide nodded, with quizzical looks.

"But trace your fingers in the soil, and see what you find."

The SS officers knelt and began to scrape for a Resistance cache.

Erwin silently unholstered his pistol. The muzzle touched the aide's head and Erwin pulled the trigger. Brain and skull fragments splattered the turf as the man fell lumpishly forward.

Major Pelz jumped and made a startled "Oh!" The major leaned on one arm, shuddering with the shock of his aide's shooting and the gore beside him on the ground.

"Major Pelz, I believe I must kill you before you kill me."

The major moved his arms as if wanting to push away reality, or perhaps to stretch time.

"Major Pelz, I once believed any sacrifice for the Fatherland was noble." Erwin searched Pelz's face. "I can imagine you believe this still."

The young major nodded slowly. Erwin saw that the little interrogation was going to be useless, that Pelz would speak any words or make any face that would induce Erwin to spare his life.

Erwin prolonged the questions a little, anyway. "But life never forced you to confront that belief in the concrete. In this respect, you're unlike me." And unlike Colonel Schussler, he thought.

Major Pelz's face betrayed nothing.

"And you believe it's right to sacrifice others. Not only resisters, but Jews, for example."

Major Pelz tried not to cry. "I'm afraid you are more the philosopher than I, Colonel Schell. I have instructions. I didn't create whatever it is that upsets you so." Major Pelz made a child's face, as if hoping his piteous look would evoke some recognition.

So this, Erwin thought, is what the Third Reich is reduced to: launderers and clerks. Compared to his predecessor Colonel Schmidt, Major Pelz was even more alarming: an automaton. Surely, Erwin thought, there was no such thing. He tried again to "look behind Pelz's eyes," as he had heard the locals say, to find some spark of common humanity. But Pelz's eyes had nothing to say. Nothing but panic.

"You would have been safer to fight the Nazis from the start. I'm sorry, Major Pelz."

He fired into the major's face. Pelz lurched backward, showing no experience of pain, his maimed head falling onto the aide's chest.

Erwin found no blood on his own clothes. He stepped out of the woods into the clearing, saw Zimmer approaching, and fired the rest of his clip at random targets. Seeing Erwin at target practice, Zimmer turned around. Then Erwin holstered his pistol, hurried to the sewing-room door, and knocked.

Sophia opened it warily.

"I've just shot two SS men who came to arrest you. They're lying in the woods by the path; they'll be easy to find. The Farm Inspector can find some way to remove them. I can occupy Nagel and Zimmer for half a day; then the bodies must be gone."

He spoke without pausing, giving Sophia no chance to interrupt and deny her connection with the Farm Inspector. By the time Erwin had finished, she had stopped trying.

"Alright," she answered.

"The best place to drop the bodies would be just outside a combat zone of the Arnhem battle. Make sure their identifications are on them so they're accounted for. We don't want to draw down another SS investigation. They say Americans are shooting SS as they find them. Maybe the British are, too, so no one should be shocked to find these two shot at point blank."

Erwin took Nagel and Zimmer to check for infiltration routes. He watched Zimmer and Nagel search intently for signs of enemy reconnaissance; then Erwin's mind turned to his new status. To the extent that he had any relation to the Third Reich at all, it was the relation of outlaw. Outlaw -- the term was fair, he thought. He had moved outside the Third Reich's law. No, a better word was the Third Reich's lawlessness. He had reestablished justice. He had judged Major Pelz, pronounced sentence, and given the sentence execution.

Pelz's motivations he understood perfectly: an unconsidered love for country, and a deference to men he respected. That was no defense. There could be no safe haven from the responsibility of thought.

By seeking to kill Sophia, the SS had forced him to choose. Erwin had chosen.

Despite the deepening cold, Erwin looked for things to do outside. He knew that his devotion to Germany, and the stream of honors he had won, had filled some hole in his spirit. Now the hole lay exposed, like a nerve in a decayed tooth. The anger he had cultivated his whole career against Communists to the east, against capitalists to the west, the anger that fueled his soldiering, found no outlet, and worked instead inside him, like a parasite he could actually feel, depleting him. Many times he imagined taking relief with a good *jenever*. But he knew the parasitic anger would return, possibly worse than before, and he overcame the lure of a drink.

In motion he found relief, outside, with Sophia's children. He took Geertruide riding, and the anger slept while the horses moved. Dismounted again, he felt the parasite chewing again.

The shallow canal at the back of Paardenveld froze early, and Erwin took the children skating every day. At the ice's edge he tugged their skate laces snug, then as the children sailed away he laced his own and followed, free and ageless on the frozen canal. Later, walking back to Paardenveld, he felt the parasitic anger.

One morning, coming back from the ice, he followed Geertruide absently into the sewing room as she put away her skates. Sophia sat by a newly-mounted easel, her black hair curling onto a white smock.

"Too cold to paint in the greenhouse?" Erwin asked.

Ignoring his question, Sophia said, "I want to paint you."

"Why?"

"I've never painted a person before, never been sure what I'd show. With you, I think I know."

What on earth was the right thing to say? Before he could even say the wrong thing, Sophia spoke again. "Not in your uniform."

To Erwin, it felt as if a different person, not Erwin, were removing his tunic and sitting motionless while Sophia, the most seeing person he had ever met, gave her full attention to him and began to express in paint what she saw. As the time passed, he settled into his pose and his tension dissolved into curiosity: what was taking shape on the canvas, turned away from his view?

Finally she said, "It's almost ready. But you shouldn't see it till I've finished."

Erwin rose wordlessly, pulled his tunic from the hook and left the room.

The next morning Sophia met him when he finished his breakfast, led him back to the sewing room, lifted the canvas and held it to his view. For a full minute, his gaze moved over this portrait of himself. Under the dried oil, the cheeks' color betrayed a warmth Erwin often felt, but had never imagined anyone could see.

His painted eyes seemed on the verge of a playful smile, giving the face an ageless quality. If a viewer screened the lower half of his face, he might imagine Erwin as a young child, or as an old man.

Child eyes, old-man eyes. Eyes about to smile. Soul exposed like a soft-shelled crab, protectionless. Naked and taking pleasure in the simple fact of existence, the being he had doubted he had the courage to become. Sophia had seen his possibility, exposed what he concealed. Visually roaming the painting, for the first time he felt unalone, conscious of the profoundest friendship. This extraordinary woman. He knew, more certainly than he had ever known anything in his life, that his love for her had not been a sickness at all.

"Thank you." His voice came from deep in his stomach.

He carried the painting through the hallway to his office and positioned it out of the window's glare. Alone with the picture, he lost himself in it, the way a man stares at a campfire or the ocean. Between the buttons of his shirt he scratched the hairs on his chest, then fingered his ear, then pressed his hands against his hips as he gazed.

November, 1944

The sky was already dark, and the aides had gone for the day. From the side of his hospital bed Willem slid onto his crutches. Leaning on the crutches, the ankles seemed fine. But when he shifted weight to his feet, pain shot up his legs. Worse, the ankles did not lock and he lurched onto the crutches for balance. He sat again on the bed, impatient.

Outside, brakes screeched, truck doors slammed and German voices called to each other. Willem watched the door until an SS officer with a medical armband came through and switched on the dim light, illuminating his tired face like a decorated pumpkin. "Attention! We're moving patients capable of transport to Germany."

The British must be attacking again, Willem thought.

Two SS walked straight to Willem and his thoughts raced. It was unthinkable just to vanish again, without warning Sophia. Before he could finish the thought, the SS reached him. They lifted Willem as gently as they might lift one of their own and carried him out to the nearest truck bed. Moments later, an SS man returned with extra blankets. Willem spread the blankets distractedly, imagining Sophia's shock, and wondering what she would tell the children.

COINCIDENCE
December, 1944

Sophia counted days to the end of December. Even the children had not complained when they passed the Sinterklaas days with no celebration. But not celebrating only punctuated the gloom of the dark solstice which happier Christmases had brightened.

Willem had disappeared, with all the Sint Anna's patients who could be moved. No one could say where.

Sophia put her head on her pillow and heard the children breathing, fast asleep. She tried to let go of Sinterklaas, let go of Willem, let go of war, let it go, let it go.

A knock woke her. Was this the first knock, or had she heard it in her sleep and resisted? She looked toward her closed curtains and heard another tap on the glass. She folded her gown against her skin and stepped toward the window, squinting to see in the near-dark, and pulled the curtains. She lurched at the sight of a desperate man before she recognized Maarten.

Maarten gestured to open the window, glancing over his shoulder, then crouching like a hunted animal. Sophia strained to raise the window, then reached for Maarten's long arms as he thudded over the sill onto the floor.

"Shhh!" Sophia hissed. "You'll wake the Germans, or terrify the children."

Maarten's lungs pulled great chunks of air into his slender chest. Sophia closed the window and drew the curtain.

"Maarten, what is it? Did you leave the work crew? Are they hunting for you?"

He drew more air into his desperate lungs. "I ran all the way from my house. I went to check on Anna but the Gestapo's there, interrogating her right now. She has no idea where I am. She couldn't. That's why I forged the work papers and told her I was drafted for a labor crew. She couldn't know I was involved in sabotage."

Maarten sniffed loudly. "Going home was a mistake; I'm sure the Gestapo spotted me. They followed me but I don't think they saw me come onto your property."

His chest still heaved. "Sophia, you must do something for me."

"What is it?"

"Check on Anna. If they're still interrogating her, I'll surrender. But if she's safe, I'll disappear across the river."

Sophia began to change clothes, hurrying, immodest of his presence. Neither staring nor looking away as she changed, Maarten said, "Sophia, don't tell Anna I'm here. I don't want her to have that responsibility."

Dressed, Sophia said, "Follow me. You can hide in the chapel."

Sophia opened the shed as quietly as she could and wheeled out a bicycle. Ignoring the curfew, she pedaled westward on the river road in pitch dark toward Anna's house, imagining the road edge, and luckily never crossing it. She finished the ride without meeting another human. She laid the bicycle silently on the ground, tiptoed to the door and knocked. Anna opened immediately.

"Oh, Anna, I dreamed the Germans had murdered you! It was so realistic, I had to come see you alive."

Anna's white face was flush now and pink. "Sophia, you won't believe it: the Gestapo were just here! They say Maarten's in the Resistance, instead of a work crew. Sophia, I've never been so afraid!"

"You must be terrified! Oh, Anna, move in with us at Paardenveld. Tomorrow. It's safe there."

Anna moved her hand through her blond hair. "Maybe I will."

In the chapel again, Sophia shook Maarten gently. "Maarten, wake up."

He lurched, snarling.

She pressed his chest to reassure him. "It's me: Sophia. Maarten, it's me. You're in the chapel at Paardenveld. It's all right."

A stubble darkened Maarten's careworn face. He blinked. "Sophia. You went to my house?"

"The Gestapo's gone; Anna's fine. She was terrified, but she's fine. I asked her to move in with me tomorrow."

Maarten said, "I'll cross the river tomorrow after dark."

"Is it safe?"

"There's no choice. We're struggling. Our group leader and ten of the best agents were executed before the Normandy landing. You remember Hogeboom, always wore the olive cap with a gold shield?"

"Hogeboom?"

"Your Colonel Schell had him killed after the NSB murders."

Sophia felt her chest and face tinge. "Maarten, Hogeboom was a collaborator! I saw him agree to cooperate with the Germans, right here. They caught him spying, and gave him the option of hanging or turning."

"That was an act. He meant to be captured, and only pretended to turn. Then he gave the Germans false information."

"How do you know that?"

"We planned it."

"Did you know Hogeboom told the SS I was a Jew?"

"*Verdomme*! I thought I'd convinced him . . ."

Sophia hesitated, then took the risk, trusting Maarten. "The Farm Inspector . . ."

"What about him?"

"Why didn't he know about Hogeboom?"

"We were independent, organized from Britain. We couldn't afford for other cells to know about us, in case they were infiltrated."

Sophia bit her lip. By framing Hogeboom and forging the reprisal files, she and the Farm Inspector had killed eleven patriots.

"You're pale, Sophia. I can see it even in the dark." Maarten touched her forehead. "And sweating! Sophia, what is it?"

"I have to leave. Go back to sleep; you're safe here. No one ever comes here but me." She stopped at the door. "I'll put some food inside before daylight. And tomorrow I'll come after dark to tell you it's safe to leave."

Sophia stumbled out, reeling from the news of Hogeboom and the resisters, stricken by her shattering inadequacy. She felt sure that a subconscious terror had swallowed her cognition, that she had framed Hogeboom because he had threatened to expose her past. For the first time she could remember, she could not trust her own mind, and reality seemed more than she could manage.

December, 1944

Erwin wondered what to say. He had seen Sophia unnerved before, after Colonel Schmidt's attack in Rhenen. This was different: today she looked dazed.

The children finished lunch and ran to play in the sprinkling snow that melted as it touched ground. When they were out of hearing, Erwin touched her elbows and asked, "Sophia, what's wrong?"

Their glances met only an instant, as if she could not hold eye contact with another human and keep her composure.

He spoke as reassuringly as he knew how. "There's nothing you should be afraid to tell me."

Sophia stopped scrubbing the plate in her hand and held it without speaking. Finally she said, "This war is too much for me. I'm not sure I can wait for peace to come."

She stared into the sink, and then through the window.

"Something's happened," he said. "Please tell me."

He saw that she almost spoke, and then held herself. He offered one more nudge: "No matter what, Sophia, your secret will be safe."

Her shoulders began to shake.

"Let's go sit down," Erwin said. He took her hand and led her back to the breakfast table.

Sophia looked at him, still sobbing, before she began. "Hogeboom was in the Resistance."

"I know; that's why we shot him."

Sophia laughed blackly. "The Farm Inspector and his group released Guse, then Guse helped them kill Schmidt and the NSB men in town."

"Guse helped them?"

"They burglarized Hogeboom's house and planted his clothes at the headquarters."

"Why?"

"I saw when Zimmer and Kessler arrested Hogeboom. And I saw you release him. You shot the first spy, the one who wouldn't cooperate. So when Hogeboom left alive, I knew he'd agreed to give information. I told the Farm Inspector. Hogeboom was a perfect man to frame. And we knew there'd be reprisals. If someone had to die, why not get collaborators killed? So the Farm Inspector forged the list for you to find, the ten you arrested and turned over for execution. We made the list from people we thought were helping the Germans. But they were all resistance. They all died because of information I gave the Farm Inspector; that started the whole plan."

"That's what's bothering you?"

Tears wetted her red cheeks.

"You're this upset because eleven people died?"

Sophia was silent.

"Sophia, do you have any idea how many people are dying in this war? Babies, children, mothers and grandmothers, old men who just want to be left alone? A fighter pilot kills ten times that number of his own neighbors, just downing a bomber."

Sophia just looked out the window, shuddering.

Suddenly he understood: it was something even worse than the deaths: a paralyzing self-doubt, attacking this extraordinary woman who used her mind more ably than anyone he knew.

"Sophia, you based a conclusion on what you saw. That's all rational people do. These are insane times. You have to let yourself be wrong without losing faith in your mind."

Sophia put her fist against her mouth and shivered as she spoke. "Can you find Willem for me?"

"Willem?"

Sophia looked into his eyes a very long time.

"My husband. He was part of the Arnhem parachute jump. He broke his ankles and was recovering at the clinic. A few weeks ago I went there and he was gone; I've been frantic to know where they took him."

"God in Heaven," Erwin let the words escape softly. Sophia's husband. He caught himself staring and said, "I'll find him."

Sophia did not move her eyes from him. "And bring him to Rhenen?"

"No. I couldn't guarantee his safety. Some of the beaten Germans will be vengeful. Some will think themselves victims as so many did after the last war."

He looked out the window, and spoke as if to himself. "There's nothing more dangerous than a victim; someday victims will destroy the World."

He faced Sophia. "I'll take him to a crossing where he can meet the Canadians. When this area's liberated, he can reach you safely. I'll stay with you till the Germans are all gone."

December, 1944 - January, 1945

The model patient rose again and shifted his weight from the crutches to his feet. No pain now. And his ankles braced like healthy joints; the alarming give was cured. He danced slightly to get the feel of full movement again, to test the ankles' limits.

The time was coming to think about escape. He sat again on his bed and waited for dinner, trying to remember the escape kit the British had given him for his jump: compass, map, local currency. What had he done with them? He wondered how he might get civilian clothes.

The German staff talked excitedly and hovered near the radio; "Belgium" came into their conversation over and over.

"What is it?" Willem asked the seventeen-year-old who carried his tray of broth and bread. "What's all the excitement?"

The aide spoke as if Willem were a fellow German. "We've launched a counterattack, with tanks and planes and artillery, as big as the force that took France in 1940. We've already taken a hundred thousand prisoners. We may retake Antwerp in a week; in two weeks, we may reach the Atlantic."

Willem rolled his eyes. "Who says that? The propaganda radio?"

The attendant's face clouded. After a moment he shrugged and left Willem's lonely supper.

On Christmas Eve the staff sang carols before going home, leaving two forlorn guards.

Over the next dreary week, talk of Belgium died; the German counterattack must have withered. But the good news cheered him only a little: how had his family spent such a cold December, without him?

On New Year's Day a *Wehrmacht* colonel entered his ward. The colonel's very appearance commanded attention, a historical figure, or a character in some drama, with the alertness of a man who had confronted great challenges, but with eyes deep-set from some inexpungible sadness. The colonel spoke quietly to the nurse, who pointed toward Willem.

The colonel strode over. "*Dokter Van Dordrecht?*"

"*Ja?*" Willem answered.

The colonel studied him, as if comparing him to a photograph, then extended his hand. "I'm Colonel Erwin Schell. My headquarters is at your house."

Willem felt his face go flush.

"I'm here to release you."

"Why?"

"Sophia asked me to."

Willem felt a pointed anger. He knew Germans did not casually use first names, so why did this colonel use Sophia's? The colonel was nearly finished before Willem began to listen to his words again.

"But I think your safety requires that you go back across the river for now. Some Germans are bitter, dangerous. You're safer on the other side until this is over."

"Is my family safe?"

"Don't worry, I have two good men still there. We won't leave them till this is over, one way or the other."

The colonel looked around. "Do you have anything to take with you?"

"Not really. Only what I'm wearing."

Willem walked to the entrance unsupported, and grimaced as he stepped into the January sunlight. The colonel led him to an American jeep with canvas top and stood by the passenger door, ready to help him climb in, but Willem took no help. The colonel stepped around, mounted nimbly, started the engine and put the jeep in gear.

Willem asked, "This is American, isn't it?"

"A glider crashed behind our lines at Arnhem, with this inside."

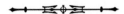

They rode twenty minutes. It would have been rude to stare, but Erwin glanced many times at the younger man beside him, curious to know Sophia's husband. "You're a lucky man."

"Why do you say that?"

From the doctor's tone, Erwin saw that he had offended him. "Your wife's the most extraordinary person I've ever met."

"What do you mean?" The doctor's voice was more hostile than before.

"She has a mature view of what makes her happy."

"What makes her happy?"

Erwin turned. "Her children. And creating; she's the most creative person I've ever known."

Erwin looked at the road. Then he faced Sophia's husband again. "I can imagine you made her happy."

For several minutes they drove in silence. "You should have seen how she sheltered your children. She defended a townsman and gave information to the Resistance at the risk of her own life. She's been loyal to you, to your family, to her country."

The doctor made a face of disbelief. "You knew she was helping the underground and permitted it?"

"The time came when I had to choose."

They rode in silence again.

"I must tell you, Doctor van Dordrecht, that I looked many times at your photograph and wondered whether you deserved such a wife."

The doctor spoke slowly. "Sorry, but your thought was not especially original. I wondered the same thing."

Erwin spoke evenly. "After the war I'll ask Sophia to choose. You asked my motive for keeping you safe. Now you know."

He saw the younger man's face go red, and a vein in his forehead protrude in anger. "If she chooses a Nazi, she deserves a Nazi. Whatever my failings, nothing could make me as guilty as you. You murdered and plundered."

Erwin listened without speaking.

The doctor went on, "Since this war began, I've saved hundreds of lives. How about you?"

Erwin measured his tone, not rising to match his rival's. "Three. Sophia van Dordrecht. Geertruide van Dordrecht. Herbert van Dordrecht."

"Would they have been in danger in the first place, except for you?"

Erwin looked directly at Willem. "Do you really think there is anything you can say to me that I don't already accept? You see us as criminals, and I understand perfectly why."

Erwin looked at the road ahead, shook his head, and made a bitter smile. His passion slowly rose as he spoke. "I doubt you can ever know the sense of mission we had. Now I see how ridiculous it was, how much suffering . . ."

After a moment Erwin remembered himself and finished. "Now I'm correcting the damage as best I can. That's the second reason you're sitting beside me."

The jeep hummed up to the Rhine checkpoint. Erwin waited for the guard to recognize his colonel insignia and his *Pour le Mérite*. He knew the guard's thoughts as he recognized the medal: that he was in the presence of a hero of the Third Reich. But Erwin felt like a spy.

The guard saluted with vigor and Erwin returned the salute. "*Guten morgen, Korporal.* This patriotic Netherlander was attached to the American infantry as a double agent. I'm returning him for further duties. He'll pretend to escape. Is there a point where he can cross without being observed?"

"There are some skiffs a hundred meters downstream. He could take one of those."

"My question was, where can he board without being noticed?"

"I'm sorry, Colonel, that's what I meant. The Netherlanders take their boats out to fish. They never try to cross, so we don't interfere. The Canadians would likely stay calm if he used one of those boats. Or I could fire at him, to give the impression of an escape."

"That might raise more alarm than we want. *Danke, Korporal.* I'll take him to the skiffs."

They walked downstream toward the boats. Erwin said, "It will ruin your incognito if I stay with you. So this should be goodbye."

Willem said, "I think I have two things to say."

"What are those?"

"For anything you did for my family, I give my absolute thanks." Erwin accepted the proffered hand, and the handshake lingered, each thinking of the other's words, his way of carrying himself, his look of hardships overcome.

As they ungripped hands, Erwin asked, "What's the second thing?"

"Whatever you did for them, you still invaded my country and took my property. I was unprepared and did nothing to prevent it. You'll never know how much I regret that. That's the last time in my life that will happen. If we ever meet on my property, my aim will be to kill you."

Erwin only smiled. It was a smile of respect and recognition, the smile of a man about to become old.

"*Vaarwel, Dokter Van Dordrecht,*" Erwin said in his best Hollandish.

Willem turned his steps toward the boat he was about to steal.

Willem gripped an empty paint can on the bank and dipped into the near-frozen water sloshing two inches deep in the bottom of the boat. His weight tipped the boat, sending the leak-water back to make a pond around his feet. The can stirred the scum and clouded the clear water; his fingers holding it quickly went numb. When the boat was nearly dry, he threw the paint can back to shore, chose a small board as an oar, then pushed off.

The colonel was gone.

His hands blistered as he paddled hard with the board. The boat leaked again, and he wished he had kept the paint can for bailing. When he left the stern seat and knelt in the bottom to paddle, his pants soaked up the frigid leak-water.

At last his bow hit the far shore. The current swung the stern till his starboard lined the water's edge. Willem clambered out, clunking the board loudly on the hull, clasped the painter and pulled the nose up the bank.

Three Canadians met him, raw men with new-shaven faces, faces without the veterans' lines of fear and exhaustion. Faces like the Americans before Normandy.

One clasped Willem's upper arm; another covered him with a pistol as they led him up the riverbank.

"State your business" was the first thing one of them said, full of suspicion, as if Willem were Hitler's trusted agent.

He sat in their camp without identification, shivering under the blanket they offered, wondering how he would explain his release by a German colonel in love with his wife. Then a familiar voice called out. "Well, I'll be damned! The Flying Dutchman!"

Willem turned to see Buster Lindell and his face warmed with relief. Then John Hightower appeared. Willem rose quickly and shook their hands hard.

Hightower faced the Canadians. "Where'd you find this man?"

"He crossed the river. You know him?"

Hightower said, "Dutch Army surgeon. Landed with us on D-Day. Left our squad to make the Arnhem jump; must have been captured and escaped. Is that what happened?" They looked at Willem.

"That's the short version."

The youngest and most serious Canadian challenged Hightower. "No one from the German side fired at him. What makes you so sure he's not a spy?"

"He's not smart enough to be a spy," Lindell intervened.

A second Canadian, his eyes narrowing, picked up his weapon. "Just a minute. How do we know these two" -- gesturing at Lindell and Hightower -- "aren't spies?"

Hightower spoke with an edge, as if the wrong answer would provoke him to pull a weapon. "Goddammit, how do we know you aren't spies?"

"Forget it, John, the jig is up." Lindell raised his hands in mock surrender. "You Canajuns was just too sharp for us."

The youngest Canadian scowled, but the other two laughed. One said, "You want him? Sending him back to your unit is easier for us. Otherwise we have to process him."

"Sure. We'll take him off your hands and give you this case of smokes, if you can spare some kerosene."

Willem put on a dry set of Canadian fatigues, then helped load the kerosene into the deuce-and-a-half. He crowded into the front with Lindell and Hightower, warm and happy as the truck bounced on the rutted road. He told the story of his capture, and his release by the German colonel living with his wife and children.

"Lordy Day," Lindell mused. "This war."

> *I walked up to a brakeman*
> *To give him a line of talk.*
> *He said "If you've got money,*
> *I'll see that you don't walk."*
>
> *"I haven't got a nickel.*
> *Not a penny can I show."*
> *"Get out, get out! You railroad bum!"*
> *He slammed the boxcar doe.*
>
> *Yo ho dee odlee oh ho dee odlee odee oh, hee*
> *Yo da ladee, ho, dee odlee hee.*

Lindell yodeled the rest of the way. As they pulled into the clearing, Willem saw the little knot of his friends.

259

Mad Jack Haggerty hurried over. "*There's* the workin' girl's friend. Someone go find Major Brady!"

Hightower hurried off.

Ichinowski's goofy lips spread in a wide grin. "Goddammit! We thought you were going to liberate Denmark."

"Holland."

"Well it looks like you blew it." Ichinowski's grin widened. "Can't you do anything right?"

Lindell said, "Hold on, Ron, I think we all know a Dutchman's harder to liberate than a Frenchman. We've seen that ourselves."

"That's a useful piece of analysis."

Haggerty just stared, as if there would be no end to the strangenesses this war would bring.

Brady followed Hightower into the clearing, walking fast. "Father, Son and Holy Ghost. That was a nasty business you signed up for."

Willem told his story again, till Brady said, "Jesus H. Christ. So here you are."

Willem looked at Brady's new insignia. "So you're a major now."

"That's no great honor. You know how officers get promoted."

"I'm surprised to see you this far north."

It was only after the adrenaline had faded that Willem noticed how bad they looked. The creases from their eyes bent down. It seemed it would be rude to show happiness in their presence, and they looked fiercer, as if only a small provocation could set them off.

March, 1945

"We've crossed the Rhine."

"When?"

"Yesterday, at Remagen. A hundred Americans crossed a railroad bridge."

"A bridge that wasn't blown? We control it?"

"We must. The company's heading south to cross."

Did the bridge sway and tremble? Or was it only the strangeness of the Germans leaving it intact, that made the trestle seem so tenuous? Willem stepped uncertainly until his boot touched the solid east bank.

"We're not sure where the front is," Brady said, "so we'll probe the farm road northeast till we meet resistance."

Willem glanced back at the Rhine. With anything to float on, he might have ridden the current home in a few hours.

Instead they moved ahead in a gathering mist. Maybe an hour passed before Ichinowski pointed to a church spire just over the treetops. "Hold up." Haggerty unfolded his map. "I think that must be Dixenheim. On the map it looks like not much more than a railroad crossing with a cathedral."

As they moved forward, the spire sank below the tree-line out of view.

"What's that?"

"What's what?"

"Sounds like shouting."

"Heads up!" Haggerty warned the others.

"Combat troops wouldn't make that kind of noise."

"Double-time," Haggerty said. "Heads up."

Through the drizzle they trotted into view of the town. In the square, a burning warehouse illuminated the mist's dullness like a florescent bulb in an evil dream. Villagers shouted around it. At the sight of Americans trotting in with weapons ready, the crowd broke up in confusion.

"*Was ist das?*" Willem asked someone.

"Resisters. Jews."

Willem looked at the villager's face for a sign he had misunderstood, but seeing none he dropped his weapon and shoved through the crowd to the warehouse, ignoring the heat that burned his eyebrows and nostrils. At the door the heat was so strong it blew him physically backward, until he leapt forward anyway and flung the bolt upward. Touching the bolt, his palm seemed to burn all the way into the bones before his hand went numb. The bolt slipped back into the lock as he fell backward, swooning from heat, conscious of screams from the still-living inside.

Someone pulled him away. Looking up he saw Forrest Hall's face. With his ears ringing, Willem thought he imagined the Americans slinging buckets of water uselessly against the inferno.

Through the ringing in his ears, Willem heard Brady barking to him. "Can you talk? We need a translator."

Willem stumbled toward them.

"This is the mayor," Brady said. "That's all I can understand."

The pale mayor trembled. "I am Herman Stresse, the Burgemeister."

"What happened?"

"It was a relocation train from Holland. Your bombers destroyed the rail just ahead, so the guards kept the prisoners cooped up until they could move again. It was too long in there without food, and after two days the prisoners tried to escape. The guards shot the leaders, but the train still could not move. So the guards put the rest in that warehouse."

As Willem translated, Brady's eyes grew wide with amazement.

The Burgemeister looked at the ground, and then up again. "Just before you came some of the guards set it on fire. I stood in front of the door, but no one in the square would help me."

Brady threw his helmet on the ground and kicked it. "Goddammit! What kind of people are you?"

Brady picked up his helmet and hurled it into the crowd. "You want to play with fire? Do you? I'll show you a goddamned fire! Haggerty! Elkins! Fratto!"

The sergeants ran to Brady, who stamped the ground like a bull.

"Get your flamethrowers," he said.

"What did he say?" the Burgemeister asked.

Willem did not reply, but stepped up to Brady. "No."

Brady in his rage struggled to make sentences. "What do you mean, 'no'? Enough! They brought it to the goddamned world, and we're gonna bring it to them."

Willem gripped the taller Brady, his chest in Brady's chest, using the strength of his legs to push them both away against Brady's resistance.

"No, I said." Willem hissed the words, his spittle landing on Brady's cheeks. "Those were my people. For all I know, that was my family. And I say no. You'd be just like them."

Brady resisted once more and Willem pushed him farther. "It's the one thing you did in this war you'll never get over. I'm telling you: no."

The crowd watched as Brady stopped resisting and turned to walk a jagged line away, one hand on his head, looking up at the sky.

"Thank you," the Burgemeister said to Willem, weeping like a child.

Willem shouted to the sergeants, "Put the flame-throwers away. But no one leaves till we know who did what."

Willem said in German to the Burgemeister, "Find something to write with. Get names of everyone in this square, and what each one did: who spread kerosene, who lit the fire, who cheered them on, anything. Then you sign the paper. These soldiers are going to arrest them for murder. Start now, and nobody leaves till we're finished."

"Tell me your name," the Burgemeister said.

"Willem Vaubin van Dordrecht, of Rhenen in Holland."

"I'll help you. Everyone who lives here will remember what you did."

The man with no eyebrows, Ichinowski renamed him.

For ten days Brady did not speak to him. It was worth it, Willem told himself.

On the tenth day Brady found him alone. "Willem. I got you a transfer."

Willem felt his lip curl in a bitter sneer. "Because of Dixenheim?"

Brady twisted his face. "You think I'm transferring you because you stopped me from torching a village? You were right: I never would have gotten over that."

"Then why?"

"Hell, it's really up to you. I just thought about what you said: those were your people in that warehouse. If I were you and I'd seen that, I'd go straight home. I'd find out where those trains are coming from and I'd make sure no more left." Brady paused. "I can't get you home, but I can sure get you closer than this. The Canadians have bridgeheads over the Rhine downstream at Rees and Wesel. A regiment's moving downriver toward Arnhem."

"How do I get there?"

"We'll lend you a jeep. You'll have to cross back to the Rhine's west bank. The Remagen bridge finally gave way, but we have pontoons. Then you'll cross back over to the east bank downstream."

Willem gripped Brady's hand. "Well."

Everything he might say sounded stupid. He said it anyway. "You're the best friend I've made in this war. Come to my house before you ship home. It's called Paardenveld. It's the first house west of Rhenen on the river road. Promise me."

"I'll look you up before I ship. Paardenveld?"

"It means 'horse field.' In case you forget the Dutch name. Ask someone how to say 'horse field,' then ask directions in Rhenen, ask anywhere west of Arnhem, really."

"Alan Smythe." With his handlebar mustache and chiseled face, the man putting out his hand looked like a cartoonist's vision of a colonel, or a Canadian Mounted Policeman.

"Willem van Dordrecht," Willem said as he shook hands.

Smythe looked at his map. "You're from Rhenen?"

"That's right."

"I guess you know the terrain pretty well."

"I've cycled every farm road to the German border more times than I could count."

"And of course you speak Dutch."

"I remember a little."

Smythe did not smile. "I'm putting you with the company taking downriver point. They've flooded the fields around Arnhem, so the maps are not that reliable. If you get blocked, maybe you can find a way around."

"I would think so."

"We expect a little skirmishing, nothing major. Few miles a day, careful for snipers and booby-traps. Take your jeep a kilometer downstream and ask for Captain Guest. That's Company C."

Willem estimated a kilometer and pulled the jeep over. Hoisting his kit, he stepped toward a group setting up tents, but stopped in dismay when he recognized the Canadians who had met him crossing the Rhine. He paused, then stepped toward them anyway; he wanted to get home.

"Company C?"

Seeing Willem, the Canadians stopped what they were doing. "Hey, aren't you the spy we captured in January?"

All the suspicion was gone as they put out their hands. One wore a lieutenant's bars, and the other two wore sergeants' stripes: combat promotions since January.

"Tim Jenkins," said the lieutenant.

"David Rutledge," said one of the sergeants.

"Jim Landry," said the other.

"Willem van Dordrecht."

"You can tent with us."

Willem marched alongside Jenkins. "Arnhem will be a hard fight," Jenkins said. "They won't give up another river crossing with a rail center."

Willem said, "Let's look at your map."

Jenkins stopped, opened his case and unfolded his map. Willem traced the paper with his finger. "I don't see it here, but there's a small canal with hard-topped dikes that makes a half circle. What if we just by-passed Arnhem?"

"You're ready to get home," Jenkins laughed.

"Yes, I am. But it makes sense anyway. If there's an easy by-pass, you can move downriver and set up more crossings anywhere you want."

"How do you get around Arnhem?"

Willem pointed at the map. "Once we reach this canal, we might be able to follow the dikes without being seen."

"Let me talk to Captain Guest."

Jenkins disappeared, rejoining them thirty minutes later. "I can scout your way with a platoon and report back. Captain'll decide later how big a deviation we take."

Jenkins called to Rutledge and Landry. "Get your squads, we're trying to by-pass Arnhem. Single file: Willem first, then me, then the rest of you strung out behind. Stay in sight of the man in front. Recognition signs 'Procter' and 'Gamble.' Let's hear signs."

"Procter," they chorused.

"Answer?"

"Gamble."

"Okay."

FREEDOM
March, 1945

Sophia sat alone with her sewing. For three days no Germans had passed on the road, and she let Geertruide and Herbert play outside again.

Erwin stepped in the doorway. "I think they're all gone. Germans, I mean." He said the word "Germans" as if he were not one. "NSB, too."

Sophia stood. "I haven't seen any for days."

"Well, I've kept a promise to myself: I think you're safe."

"Anna and I can move into town if necessary."

"I'll take Zimmer and Nagel to surrender. We can pass north of Arnhem and meet Canadians on the river road."

She nodded.

Erwin said, "After this is finished I'll come back."

Sophia's cheeks warmed; she wondered if she would cry. "Erwin," she said, "Willem and I will be happily married again."

"Whatever you decide, I will respect. I just want to be come back and be sure."

He stepped away as if to leave, then turned and touched her elbows. "Sophia, I'm a different person from knowing you. I feel a kind of nakedness, like an infant just out of the womb. Every sensation's new, as if everything I do, I'm doing for the first time."

He kissed her soft cheek. "Whatever happens, this is the kiss of a friend."

"A very good friend," she answered. Warm tears rolling down her face, she pulled him till he stooped, and she kissed his cheek, slowly and softly.

Erwin's voice echoed from the great hall as Zimmer and Nagel shouldered their kits.

Sophia could hear Zimmer sigh heavily. "It's a bitter thing, surrendering after so much."

Erwin's voice was soft. "That's the past, all of it. At this moment, it's the best decision."

She could only imagine their expressions, as Erwin went on. "Germany can't win; it would have been a calamity for the World if she had."

As if he knew he had not convinced them, she heard him add, "I've always said the noblest thing is to win honor, and to sacrifice for the greater good. Now I wish I could help you see that the noblest thing is to live."

Those were the last words she heard from Erwin as the heavy door closed.

"Noblest thing is to live." Erwin's words lingered in her mind. Sophia had lived, she began to accuse herself. Shared the bed of her country's enemy, while others had risked everything for conscience.

Had Marc seen it all along? Had she disowned her heritage? Somehow known the Jewish secret from childhood whisperings and disowned it at all cost? The reason she'd been so quick to marry a *jonkheer*? The reason she'd sheltered at Paardenveld with Germans when everyone else avoided them on principle?

Eleven patriots had died because she had denounced the resister Hogeboom with the olive cap. Would she have been so ready to make him the scapegoat, if he had never called her a Jew?

How clean Roos must feel, with the Germans defeated and gone. Roos, who'd never compromised.

The doorbell rang.

"Who is it?" Sophia raised her voice to be heard through the massive wood door.

"It's Anna."

In the sunlight Anna smiled as brightly as she had five Mays before. "They're all gone, Sophia. Let's go into town. Let's go remember how joy feels."

Anna bustled past her through the great hall, gathered the children and led them all outside to Paardenveld's lawn and the river road. Orange ribbons, dusted off from countless attics, laced the fences and houses. The Cunerakerk bell tower rose oddly silent, still unrepaired from bomb damage, but the church bells at Wageningen, Elst and Veenendaal rang in the distance, ringing the walkers all the way into town. From home radios playing through open windows, the melodies of *Wilhelmus* and *Oranje Boven* mingled.

Sophia felt suddenly alone, desperately apart from all these blond people whose joy was pure, so free of troubled reflections.

Anna spoke excitedly to the children and tugged her along, toward the square where a crowd was still growing. Sophia stopped, seeing some disturbance. Suddenly a handful of men emerged, pushing six women with shaved heads and painted faces. Jan Poel led them all. "*Moffenhoer!*" Each onlooker called out the word with a kick or a punch against the unprotected ribs, or a spit in the face.

"There's one!" Jan pointed at Sophia and trotted closer, the other men close behind him.

Did it last ten seconds or ten minutes? Anna lurched close in a protective hug, then was wrested away, trying again but restrained by two men, the first punches coming as Sophia bent her arms around her ribs and face for protection, but otherwise did not resist, with a strange sense of being unworthy to resist or even to feel wronged. As if her self-regard and active mind had deserted her and fled to the body of Anna, screaming like a witch and restrained by three men now, calling to Geertruide "Run! Run! Run and find the *Burgemeester!* Find the Farm Inspector!" Geertruide sprinting, passionate to save her mother who would not defend herself from the harsh shears painful against her scalp. Anna free at last and running at Jan with a loose brick but caught and restrained again. Herbert too small to matter, the men ignoring him as he pummeled them with helpless fists of tiny boy rage.

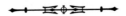

Willem and the Canadians studied a clutter of helmets just behind the dike-top.

"How many?"

"Ten or twelve."

Rutledge whispered. "So many are surrendering, maybe we just let 'em know we're here and see what happens."

Jenkins mulled this over. "How do you propose to let 'em know we're here?"

Rutledge's quiet voice came clear in the cold air. "Shoot one."

Jenkins laughed involuntarily. "All right. Set up positions on both flanks."

Jenkins turned to Rutledge. "Who's going to let 'em know we're here?"

Rutledge aimed motionless and squeezed till the rifle cracked against his shoulder. Beyond the dike-top a helmet flew backward; the other helmets ducked out of sight like alarmed birds.

"Now what?"

"Just watch."

In a moment a white flag waved, and the helmets rose again.

"I told you." Rutledge strode forward to take the surrender. "Call me Sergeant York."

Rutledge was fully exposed when, from behind the dike-top, three long-handled grenades seemed to float in the air.

"Rutledge!" Willem called out.

The grenades landed at Rutledge's feet before the sound of Willem's call had ended, three explosions tumbling the just-alarmed body, Rutledge's arms backstroking wildly with a new involuntary limberness.

Before the body touched earth, Jenkins was spitting orders. "Both sides! Go! Go! Go!"

The helmets ducked again. Without waiting for the flanks Jenkins and Willem sprinted up the middle, heaving grenade after grenade over the dike. By the time they reached the top, the grenades and the flank attacks had finished the work. Seven corpses sprawled in SS black.

Willem left the dike and knelt by Rutledge. "How are you?"

A groan escaped the twisted mouth. "Ho." His face pinched until the pupils swelled; Willem felt the pulse until he knew Rutledge was dead. Jenkins knelt alongside.

"You think they were ashamed to surrender when they saw Rutledge alone? Or do you think the white flag was a trick all along?"

"We'll never know." Jenkins still gasped for air, recovering from the sprint over the dike. "Let's make a grave. Johnson, you're the new sergeant." He shook his head.

In gathering sprinkle they walked another hour. "Where are we?" Jenkins asked.

"I think due north of Arnhem," Willem answered. "I know it by sight more than I do by direction. But I'd say due north."

They reached a new bend, where three German officer caps bobbed behind the dike top. Above the dike, a white flag fluttered on a broom handle.

Jenkins spoke just loudly enough for the squad to hear. "This close to the end, no more chances. Nobody accepts a surrender from sheltered men. Fan out, put some heat on. Kill them or flush them out."

Silently they fanned out, then approached at flank, pitching a pattern of grenades and following over the top.

Only after the flank attacks did Jenkins and Willem cross up the middle to the dike-top and view the back slope. A *Wehrmacht* colonel and two captains lay perfectly still, contorted as only grenade concussions can leave a body. Willem twisted the colonel's shoulders to see his face, and recognized Erwin Schell.

Jenkins stooped to finger the medal that dangled on the unmoving chest.

"What's that?" Willem asked.

"*Pour le Mérite*: French name, German medal. Highest honor the German military ever gave. Don't even think they still give it."

Jenkins studied the body. "He looks too valuable to be here."

"This was the colonel who released me across the river that first time I met you."

Jenkins glanced at Willem, then stared into the colonel's unblinking eyes.

"He must have planned to surrender all along."

Jenkins pulled free the *Pour le Mérite*. "He must have been something in his day."

Willem closed Erwin Schell's eyelids, then rose stiffly. "Mind if I take the medal? It's for my wife. I think they were friends."

Jenkins screwed his face. "For your wife!"

"He protected them when I was away. I know how strange it sounds. But he's not my enemy, not now."

Jenkins studied the polished multi-point cross, then handed it to Willem.

"This would have been quite a trophy. But I understand. Hell, he was a man, not a game animal."

"I doubt they would have fought us, if we'd have taken their surrender," Willem said.

"Maybe. But those SS ruined the value of a white flag."

On the flat ground at the dike's base, they dug four feet deep. They lifted Erwin Schell by the shining boots and the tunic shoulders, careful not to tear the epaulettes. They stooped to drop the body; on impact the sword sheath tapped the leg and then rested in the earth. Schell's head cocked back, extending his neck, facing the sky with open eyes.

Next they lowered the two captains. The bodies hit Schell's and shifted, rolling until they leaned against the colonel like restless sleepers. The Canadians slung the loose earth over them, then tamped the dirt mound and drifted away.

Willem and Jenkins lingered.

"No family to mourn . . ." Willem paused from phrase to phrase. "No salute from the men he led . . . No memorial of what he did or experienced on this Earth." Willem swallowed. "Just a man in the ground in the clothes that he wore."

Willem and Jenkins dropped their chins and stared at the packed dirt, then picked up their weapons and stepped away.

The Canadians marched again, still watchful. The image of the burial stayed with Willem until he spotted an abandoned bicycle in the unclipped grass at the dike's base. It was an old make with wooden wheels, the kind Bart used to ride along the pasture tracks to check his sheep.

Willem spun the wheels. It seemed usable, except that the handlebars were out of square. He faced Jenkins. "On this I could be home in an hour, just leave my gear, carry a pistol, and hope I don't meet any Germans."

"You'll get there faster that way than walking with us."

"This may be the end of your deviation. You'd better get back."

"Maybe, maybe not. We'll poke along a little farther and see what we turn up."

Willem gripped the front wheel with his knees and twisted the handlebars to square. He straddled the seat, toed the ground and pedaled, glanced backward at the Canadians and waved, then began to retrace the familiar road, leaning forward to let the large muscles in the backs of his legs into the stroke.

His peddling was choppy. Anxiety broke the old rhythm that he had known before 1940, the rhythm that used to make cycling fast and effortless. He knew the winter had been the worst in memory; how had Sophia and the children gotten through? He stroked hard but clumsily until the oxygen debt physically made him slow, his lungs seeming to mangle the air as he drew it in.

A distant figure grew into a uniformed German, who at fifty meters raised his arms, hands forward. "That's one of the last ones, looking for someone to surrender to," Willem thought. Unwilling to distract himself with a prisoner, Willem passed without slowing, ready to swing at the soldier if he neared. The German let him pass and Willem did not look back.

The air was odorless, no trace of cheese-making or manure; he passed no cattle or sheep in the pastures. The trees that lined the dikes in 1940 were gone, surely for firewood in the last desperate winter. But the timeless reeds at the waterline still rustled in the breeze, and from over his hunched figure, the sun still cast the same shadow.

Far ahead on the road he saw a second man. This one walked westward, lugging a grip. From behind, Willem recognized Bart's step and yellow flannel work shirt.

"Bart!"

Bart turned to face him and his eyes changed from suspicious to bright with recognition. "*Meneer!*"

Willem stopped the bicycle, and Bart gripped his biceps. The dairyman looked worn, some of his old energy gone.

"Bart, how are Sophia and the children?"

"I've no idea; I'm just now coming home from a labor squad."

Willem blinked but did not pause to find out what Bart meant. "Climb on. I'll pedal us both."

Bart sat over the rear wheel, his grip in his lap, arm around Willem's waist, legs out parallel to the ground like an Amsterdam girl on a date.

Willem stood on the pedals. Moving now took real effort, and he sweated in the cold spring air. He pedaled upright to Grebbeberg's summit, then sat again as the road leveled, into Rhenen and over its empty streets.

At last they cleared the western city wall, pedaled into view of Paardenveld and turned into the circular gravel driveway. Bart leapt off as Willem slowed. Willem let the bicycle drop, then strode to the front door and opened it.

In the front hall Sophia and Anna sat with the children. His eyes adjusting to the dim, he saw Sophia's hairless scalp, bruised and cut. At the sight of him she rose, as if unaware of her own strange appearance. *"Even kijken, kinderen! Hier is jullie vader!"*

Anna stood with a strange, defiant look, unsuited to her soft face.

Willem found himself next to Sophia, clasping her shoulders, harder than he had intended. "What happened to you?"

Sophia only scowled.

Willem looked to Anna, who drew her breath in sharply, as if in pain, to tell Sophia's story. "Her neighbors shaved her head, Willem. Shaved her head and beat her in front of your children. They didn't know Sophia was in the Resistance but she was. Ask the Farm Inspector."

Willem felt the near-bursting anger he'd felt at Marc's apartment in Paris. "Which neighbors?"

Sophia broke her silence. "Forget it. It's over."

Anna said, "Jan was the leader."

Impossible. "Anna, don't say that if you're not sure."

"I was there. Just yesterday."

"Why didn't Maarten stop them?"

"Maarten isn't home yet."

Willem turned to leave, his mind already on the Poel house in town; it was as if someone else were speaking as the words left his mouth. "Anna, will you stay a little longer? Look," he waved distractedly. "Here's Bart."

Willem touched his holstered pistol as he trotted out and mounted the bicycle.

Five minutes took him through town to the Poel house, where, through the broad front window, he could see the family sitting. He twisted the doorknob but a deadbolt resisted his push, so he skipped back to the bicycle and heaved it through the window with a glittering crash. He tapped away a jagged point of glass and vaulted over the sill.

Every Poel inside looked up in alarm, Jan rising from his chair. Willem reached Jan in an instant and cracked his fist across Jan's cheekbone, blooding Jan's face and Willem's own knuckles. He gripped Jan's shirt collar and belt, and slammed him to the wall, their faces only an inch apart.

"All the time I was away, all that time . . ." the words choked in his throat. "All the time I couldn't give a father's love, a husband's reassurance -- all that time -- I told myself that surely, anything he could do for my family, Jan Poel would do."

He pulled the pistol from its holster and stuck the steel mouth against Jan's cheek, next to the nose.

Eyes rolling back, Jan moved his face from the steel barrel.

"If you came here to kill me in front of my family, I can't stop you," Jan began, not masking his rage and contempt, even in the pistol's face. "You think I spent these years a gentleman banker, looking after the families of absent neighbors? I fought, Willem."

Jan nearly spat the words. "While Maarten stayed home and you ran away, I fought. I spent months in a prison camp. Then when the British came near I was interned again. In my rage I told my own son to join the Resistance. Look at him there."

Willem turned and saw Bernard in a wheelchair.

He looked at Roos, his ribs still heaving from anger and exertion. "What happened?"

But Roos was too hysterical to answer.

Jan answered instead, his voice still rising. "They caught Bernard delivering a radio and beat him up. He's crippled."

Bernard's pathetic face overruled any words. Bernard, the boy Willem had left five years before, who had called Willem "uncle," now paralyzed, beaten into half a person.

To think of killing Jan was ridiculous. But Willem's emotions lagged his conscious mind; his adrenalined hands could not let go and he held Jan against the wall silently. As the anger finally cooled, what remained was worse, a painfulness with no outlet. He slipped the pistol's safety catch and holstered it.

"Jan," he said, trying to regain his calm. "Sophia used her place at Paardenveld to help the Resistance. Anna says the Farm Inspector knows everything."

"The Farm Inspector?" The name brought a look of recognition, and Jan's face sagged. "Willem, where have you been? These years have been unbelievably hard."

Jan began to look again like his old best friend. "Jan," Willem began, hearing his own voice slowly lose its edge. "I followed Queen Wilhelmina to England; we all thought we'd come right back to fight again. Then as the time passed, I thought I might never get home."

Willem looked again at the wheelchair. "Poor Bernard."

He stepped toward their daughter on the sofa, seeing her terror. No matter what words he used, he knew she saw a wild man. "And you, Cornelia, I'm sorry I scared you. These crazy times made your father and me think we were enemies."

He moved his hands over her hair, but felt unbelievably awkward. "We were wrong. We are all friends."

Cornelia tried to nod but still shivered with fear from his touch.

"It's over, Cornelia," he tried again. "It's all over. Nothing bad will happen now."

Willem moved away, alarmed to see how his presence terrified her.

Willem gripped Bernard's hands. "Bernard, I don't understand your injuries. But this war taught doctors a lot; I know some in England who might make you good as new."

He passed Roos. "I'm sorry." Roos tried to smile but only wept.

"Jan, you'll never know how I looked forward to this day. But look how I'm spending it, fighting my oldest friends." Willem shook his head and tried to keep back tears. "I've hardly said hello to my own family."

At the door he said, "I'll come back tomorrow to help you with the window."

Jan nodded.

All the way home, Willem felt the kind of pain that a hand frozen numb feels when it begins to thaw. It was all so much worse than he'd imagined. The invasion had been like a stabbing; it made a gash but the knife was gone, and any surgeon could treat it. The occupation was different, like a cancer setting the tissue against itself. Occupation would take a shrewder doctor to heal.

No more fighting, he thought. That's not what Sophia needs; she had tried to tell him that. He wondered if he had learned anything, leaving his family the moment he saw them.

Anger lapped at his emotions like waves against a ship until his father's words came: "Sometimes anger is just the sadness you won't let yourself feel."

Just feel the sadness instead, he thought. Let it out and get ready; maybe greater challenges lie ahead than behind.

At Paardenveld, everyone still sat waiting, just the way Willem had left them.

"Willem!" Sophia looked horrified. Only now did he notice the splattered blood on his clothes.

"Jan's all right. I threw my bicycle through his window and bloodied his nose. That was before I saw Bernard. Did you know the Nazis crippled little Bernard?"

Sophia was dazed, barely acknowledging what he said.

Sophia was not the woman he had left that winter. He kept talking anyway, not knowing what else to do but share the thoughts that crowded his mind. He looked into her eyes to be sure of her attention. Did any of this make any sense to her? He rose and paced around.

"I promised Jan I'd come back tomorrow and help repair his window. More likely I'll give Bart money for a new one, and pay him to install it. And I'll send a list of English orthopedists for Bernhard."

Willem shrugged and looked upward. "But will we spend time with them again? Will they really want to? Will we try to be friends again, but not know how? I can imagine we'll speak well of each other, and be polite when we meet. But will we ever be guests in each other's houses? I can't see that far ahead."

He looked down at his fatigues. He had not bathed in many days. Neither, evidently, had Bart. Both of them had the sweetish smell of really dirty clothes.

Willem wanted to say so many things. He wanted to say he felt reborn, the object of a miracle. He wanted to tell his children how proud he was of them, that they would never live through an experience this difficult again.

Instead he said, "Herbert, do you still play *voetbal*?"

Herbert nodded.

"What position?"

"I like to score goals."

"Well, I always loved to play defender. Will you show me what you can do?"

Herbert nodded again.

"Right now? Where's your ball?"

"I'll get it."

"I'll meet you on the front lawn."

He looked at Sophia. "Come with us. Please."

"Let me get a scarf to put over my head."

He stood alone with Geertruide. Geertruide: soft as a doll, unchanging as flint. She had always been transparent to him, like a little-girl copy of himself. "Geertruide, you have the same bright, gray grown-up eyes. I remembered your eyes the whole time I was away. When I worried about you, I thought to myself: if any little girl can be all right with her father away and strangers all around, it would be Geertruide, intelligent and strong."

Geertruide started to cry.

"Geertruide, I want to sit down with you for hours, and hear all the things you've done and seen while I was away. Can we do that?"

Geertruide nodded.

"But now, Geertruide, I have a son who doesn't even know me, doesn't know or trust his own father. When I was in the hospital, you ran to me and hugged me, but did you see how your brother held back? He was too little when I left. Will you understand if I play with him first, and talk to you alone later?"

Geertruide nodded again.

"And, Geertruide, will you sit on the front lawn with your mother while Herbert and I play? I can't stand not having you where I can see you, while I'm waiting for us to talk."

Geertruide clasped Willem's hand, and he let her lead him outside.

May, 1945

The radio reports followed each other quickly. Russia's Red Army had reached the heart of Berlin, and Hitler was a suicide. Admiral Donetz would sign an unconditional surrender on May 8. In Wageningen that same day, Prince Bernhard would accept the surrender of all German forces still in Holland. Soon Queen Wilhelmina would fly to Den Haag.

Before she recognized his features, Sophia knew Guse's frame and stride, walking with a stranger.

Guse nearly lifted her off the ground. "I didn't recognize you with your scarf and short hair ..." He squinted as if he were about to ask what had happened, but did not; and Sophia did not say.

"Where did you hide this past year?" she asked. Before he could answer, Sophia turned and called. "Willem! Come see who it is!"

Willem hurried toward them.

"Willem, this is Reinhard Guse, Colonel Schell's adopted son. He fought the SS when they attacked Herbert, and had to go into hiding."

"Well, your wife saved my life, getting me a doctor after your farm man pitch-forked me. Later she arranged my protection and hiding." He smiled. *"Ik was een onderduiker."*

"Well." Willem looked upward into the taller Guse's eyes and shook his hand. The two men looked at each other in something like the way that Willem and Erwin had, standing together by the river.

"Where will you go now?"

Guse's escort introduced himself, "Aernout van Es," offering a hand, then answered for Guse. "We'll make sure the Allies know his history. He'll be a prisoner of war just long enough to be processed, and then released. Don't worry, we'll put him in a German uniform; the other prisoners will never know he joined us."

"What then?"

"Well," Guse began, "I'm thinking of going to America." He looked again to Sophia. "But first I'd like to find my father."

Sophia pulled the *Pour le Mérite* from her pocket and held Guse's hands. "Colonel Schell is dead, Reinhard. Willem saw him die, trying to surrender with Nagel and Zimmer. The Canadians thought the surrender was a trick."

"He tried to surrender?"

"He changed, Reinhard. He told me that General Langer was part of a plot to assassinate Hitler. When Langer took poison, your father completely lost faith."

Willem cleared his throat. "The grave's just a few kilometers east. He's buried without a coffin. Maybe we can move the body to a proper cemetery. Anyway, I can show you the grave."

They looked at Aernout.

"We can go there now," Aernout answered. "Then I really have to find a uniform and surrender him. I'm needed in a lot of places; there's a lot to clear up."

Guse looked at the ground, and stood with his muscles unflexed; it seemed the wind could have blown through him unimpeded. Under his breath he said, "This was the burial they gave to Hektor, breaker of horses."

Willem thought his mind was playing tricks when he saw Brady on the river road. Among the Americans he recognized Mad Jack Haggerty, then Ichinowski, Lindell, Hightower, Hall and Douglass. He greeted them almost with violence, hugging them until they pulled away, or double-gripping their hands to shake.

"How far into Germany did you go?"

"Not much farther than you last saw us," Brady answered. "We ship out of Antwerp day after tomorrow."

"Going where?"

"Not sure yet."

"I'm so glad you came this way. I want you to meet Sophia and the children!"

Beneath her scarf, Sophia's hair was as short as the Americans.' Her eyes squinted as she tried to smile. How she must seem to them, Willem thought: so different from the woman I described.

"It's an honor to meet you," Brady said to her.

She looked as if managing the conversation were a strain. "It's an honor to meet the men Willem marched with."

"I had always imagined that if I ever hosted you at Paardenveld, I'd give you a feast," Willem told them, "but there's nothing left. People were eating tulip bulbs, and old potato plantings just a week ago."

Brady gestured toward the jeep. "We can feast on powdered eggs and Hershey bars."

On May 10, Willem listened to Brady's matter-of-fact farewell.

"Tomorrow you leave for Antwerp," Brady told the men. "I'd predict you're going home. You may even be demobilized. But I won't be with you. I've been reassigned to train a new company in the Pacific."

Watching the men pack their gear, Willem just listened, savoring the familiar odd speech one last time.

"I don't know what I'll do without forty pounds on my back. Probly walk crooked the rest of my life."

"Make no mistake: next time you see me with one of these on, you'll be dreamin.'"

"Some sad character mindin' his own business'll get called up and find this stuff waitin' for him in Borneo."

Listening to them, combat seemed so far away.

"What're you gonna do your first day back?"

"Take a bath."

"That'll be a red-letter day."

"How 'bout you?"

"I'll probably be overwhelmed by the crowd cheering me at the station and break down," Ichinowski answered.

"No one'll recognize you, disguised as a soldier."

At last they were finished. "All right," Willem said. "I want a photograph."

The Americans jostled until Haggerty called them "sugared-up schoolboys" and bossed them into a formation, close enough to shoot in one frame. Just as he had with his M-1, Willem squeezed out his breath and held still to steady the picture.

Willem and Bart pushed carts to help carry their gear to the station, as Geertruide and Herbert skipped along behind. They all drank coffee on the platform and ignored the wind blustering their fatigues, until at last it was time to board.

"Okay, Willem. Nice soldierin' with you," Hightower said.

"Don't take any wooden nickels," Lindell advised.

"Good luck," said Hall.

"Say goodbye to Mrs. VD," Ichinowski added.

"I'll write you," Douglass promised.

"Steer clear of jezebels," Haggerty parodied himself, like a comic actor bowing at curtain call.

"All right," Brady said with his hand extended. "All right."

The next morning, gray and misty, it was hard to imagine the Americans had ever been there. Bart and Anneke worked again in Paardenveld's dairy. Maarten and Anna were coming for dinner.

Willem thought of the townsmen who had shaved Sophia's head, then of the pains those same ones had felt. He thought of the Germans who had taken his property, but protected his family. He muttered half-aloud, "The world has more demand for forgiveness than capacity."

Already it surprised him how much pleasure he took in his children, admiring their little bodies and movements, savoring each new thought he had not imagined them capable of. It was only Sophia who worried him now.

"Let's walk on the dike," he said to her.

Without answering, Sophia donned her scarf. Slowly they crossed the river road and climbed the sloped dike.

They walked a long time in silence, until Willem took Sophia's hand and said, "It's going to get better. You just need time."

Getting no answer, he looked squarely at her. "Sophia, we're going to live happily ever after."

Sophia scowled. "Like a fairy tale? No problems? No pain?"

"No, like real life, with problems, and pain. But using our minds to make the best of things, always."

Sophia looked at Willem, then held him tightly, blotting his shirt with the water of her tears. She shook. Her face became ugly from the trembling of her lips, as five years' anxieties found their way out. Willem held Sophia as she pressed her soft face to the shirt against his chest, shaking and expressing pain.

Acknowledgments

I thank the municipal government of Rhenen for background materials and a tower tour in the Cunerakerk. Thanks particularly to Mr. Bert Huiskes, curator of Museum Het Rondeel in Rhenen, for reviewing the text for local and linguistic fidelity. Deviations remain, to accommodate the fictional plot.

There was no German recruiting center at Rhenen, although the Germans operated a training center for Marines near Ede, a few kilometers to the northeast.

Descriptions of the battle of Grebbeberg are based on interviews with Mr. Bernier Cornielje of Wageningen, whose father fought there.

The German village of Dixenheim, and the plot elements which occur there, are fictional.

Intellectual backgrounds of some German characters (see the recruiting efforts of Colonel Schell's men in the chapter *Men of History*, Colonel Schell's first speech to the recruits in the chapter *Three Seasons*, and the statements of Colonel Schmidt in the chapters *The Middle of the War* and *The Choosing*) derive in part from Dr. Leonard Peikoff's non-fiction work, <u>The Ominous Parallels</u>.

Ludwig von Mises' book <u>Nationaloekonomie</u> (referred to in Guse's letter to Colonel Schell in the chapter *French Summer*) was adapted and republished after the war under the title <u>Human Action</u>.

It is impossible to acknowledge, or even to be conscious of, every Second World War historical source. Influences include, but are not limited to, the writings of Stephen Ambrose, Winston Churchill, Martin Gilbert, General John Hackett, John Keegan, William Manchester, and Cornelius Ryan.

Hurricane Katrina destroyed records necessary to retrace and acknowledge some sources. One example is the American innovation of dropping an empty shell case in close combat (see the chapter *French Summer*). There must be others.

No acknowledgement above is intended to imply any endorsement of this novel by the named source or influence, or to transfer responsibility for content.

Many personal friends have supplied information or offered early reads and edits; these I prefer to thank privately.

For further reading see www.Jonkheerswife.com

About the Author

A native of Fort Smith, Arkansas, John F. Landrum studied English literature at Westminster College, and law at Georgetown University. After practicing law for nine years, Landrum joined a New Orleans-area manufacturing company, where he is Vice President for Business Development. Landrum was a co-founder and president of the New Orleans Young Leadership Council, president of the New Orleans Lighthouse for the Blind, and a board member of the New Orleans Museum of Art.

A lifelong amateur student of World War II history, Landrum lived in Holland from 1994 to 1997.

He is married to Martha McDermott Landrum, and is the father of Sarah and George Landrum.

www.johnlandrum.com

Jacket Design
By Frank J. Profumo

Printed in the United States
122194LV00003B/28-75/A

9 781434 317780